Node.js Blueprints

Develop stunning web and desktop applications with
the definitive Node.js

Krasimir Tsonev

[PACKT] open source *
PUBLISHING   community experience distilled

BIRMINGHAM - MUMBAI

Node.js Blueprints

First published: June 2014

Production Reference: 1060614

Published by Packt Publishing Ltd.
Livery Place
35 Livery Street
Birmingham B3 2PB, UK.

ISBN 978-1-78328-733-8

www.packtpub.com

Cover Image by Svetlana Mircheva-Tsoneva (sv_mircheva@abv.bg)

Credits

Author

Krasimir Tsonev

Reviewers

Ben Sammons

Glenn Antoine

Bojan Bižić

Andrey Kovalenko

Miguel A. Madero

Abhijeet S. Sutar

Leo Hsieh

Commissioning Editor

Julian Ursell

Acquisition Editors

Antony Lowe

Greg Wild

Content Development Editor

Sankalp Pawar

Technical Editors

Miloni Dutia

Kapil Hemnani

Mukul Pawar

Siddhi Rane

Copy Editors

Alisha Aranha

Mradula Hegde

Adithi Shetty

Project Coordinator

Sanghamitra Deb

Proofreaders

Simran Bhogal

Maria Gould

Ameesha Green

Paul Hindle

Indexers

Hemangini Bari

Tejal Soni

Production Coordinators

Manu Joseph

Alwin Roy

Cover Work

Alwin Roy

About the Author

Krasimir Tsonev is a coder with over 10 years of experience in web development. With a strong focus on quality and usability, his interests lie in delivering cutting-edge applications. He enjoys working in the industry and has a passion for creating and discovering new and effective digital experiences. Currently, Krasimir works with technologies such as HTML5 or CSS3, JavaScript, PHP, and Node.js, although he started off as a graphic designer. Later, he spent several years as a flash developer using ActionScript3 and frameworks such as RobotLegs. After that, he continued delivering, as a freelancer, full-stack web services for his clients' graphic design as well as frontend and backend programming. With the present surge in mobile development, Krasimir is enthusiastic to work on responsive applications targeted at various devices. Having lived and worked in Bulgaria, he graduated from The Technical University of Varna with a Bachelor's and Master's degree in Computer Science.

About the Reviewers

Ben Sammons is an enthusiastic programmer who, with a background in other sciences matter, has found his passion in programming, particularly asynchronous programming. He enjoys exploring complex problems and new technologies. In his spare time, he enjoys reading fiction novels and programming goofy side projects.

> I would like to thank Sanghamitra Deb for managing the project, the author for the delightful content, and all the Node.js-core contributors for starting such a fun technology, which allows books like this to be written.

Glenn Antoine is a software engineer with over 20 years of experience. By day, much of his time is spent working with C#, .NET, and MVC enterprise-level applications. By night, he devotes his time to writing Node.js- and AngularJS-based responsive web applications. As a lifelong learner, he enjoys sharing his experiences on his blog at `http://glennantoine.com`.

Bojan Bižić started programming at the age of 14, when he got his first Commodore 64. Since then, he has come a long way developing a wide range of solutions using VB6, Delphi, C, C++, LAMP, Node.js, Objective-C, DirectX, OpenGL, OpenCL, NVidia Cuda, Python, AngularJS, and .NET. He is a Microsoft Certified Solutions Developer, database administrator, professional web developer, as well as a Certified Technology Specialist who develops SharePoint solutions. Currently, he holds a Bachelor's degree in IT Management from The University of Novi Sad, Serbia.

Bojan currently lives in Germany and works for GMG GmbH & Co. KG, developing a wide range of cross-platform color management and printing solutions, using both Microsoft and open-source technologies. In his spare time, he actively participates in open source projects.

I would like to dedicate this work to my beautiful wife Olivera. She has always been the greatest support and inspiration for my work and has made me the man I am today.

Andrey Kovalenko is a software developer, team leader, and blogger. He is a member of Jaybird Marketing Group LLC, a web and mobile development firm in the United States and Ukraine. He has been working there since the inception of the company and holds a team leader position. His work includes overseeing and implementing projects on a wide variety of technologies, with emphases on JavaScript, Node.js, HTML5, and Cordova (PhoneGap). He leads several development groups, which produce products for call centers, marketing companies, real-estate agencies, telecommunication companies, and healthcare, among others. Lately, he has been focusing on learning mobile development in details. As a result, he started the BodyMotivator project, a mobile application for fitness. He is a believer in the future of JavaScript as a generic development language. When he isn't coding, Andrey likes to hang out with his family, skydive, and exercise at the local cross-fit gym. He is a healthcare enthusiast and is trying to put all his software development efforts into making life healthier.

He is also the author of the book *KineticJS Starter*, *Packt Publishing*.

I would like to express my gratitude to the many people who saw me through this book. First and foremost, I would like to thank my girlfriend Lena for her understanding, endless patience, and encouragement when it was most required. I also thank the Jaybirdians—the amazing people to whom I now dedicate much of my life. It is through their teachings, encouragement, and support that I have gained and grown. It is an incredible feeling to know that I have worked for five years already, wrote my first book here, reviewed several books, and also created my first mobile application.

Miguel A. Madero is a developer, entrepreneur, speaker, author, and open source contributor. He has been programming for fun for almost 20 years. He founded a magazine, video production, a few web companies, and a development shop in Mexico. He has worked as a software consultant for Readify, Australia, developing some of the coolest projects in the country. He moved last year to San Francisco, where he works at Practice Fusion to connect doctors, patients, and data to drive better health and save lives. On a personal note, Miguel is married and likes rock climbing, good food, and trying exploring new things.

He also has worked on the book *Professional Visual Studio 2008*, *Wrox*.

To Carina, my wife.

Abhijeet S. Sutar is a self-taught, full-stack software developer based in Mumbai, India. He is a technology and open-source enthusiast and a blogger. Having worked with enterprise middleware applications with a Java platform, he is now building real-time applications with the Node.js platform and Meteor, along with NoSQL databases MongoDB and Redis.

He finds more interest in exploring, experimenting, reading, and writing in new languages and with new technologies.

You can reach him on his blog at `http://blog.ajduke.in`, on GitHub at `http://github.com/ajduke`, or on Twitter via `@_ajduke`.

Leo Hsieh graduated from USF with a Master's degree in Web Science in 2011. He has been working as a software engineer for over two and a half years. He is an open-source JavaScript developer, interested in frontend development and Node.js. Although he is more focused on frontend development, he is able to work on backend development with Java and Python as well.

He is also a software engineer on a platform service team at PayPal, working on a developer portal for `https://developer.paypal.com/`.

www.PacktPub.com

Support files, eBooks, discount offers, and more

You might want to visit www.PacktPub.com for support files and downloads related to your book.

Did you know that Packt offers eBook versions of every book published, with PDF and ePub files available? You can upgrade to the eBook version at www.PacktPub.com and as a print book customer, you are entitled to a discount on the eBook copy. Get in touch with us at service@packtpub.com for more details.

At www.PacktPub.com, you can also read a collection of free technical articles, sign up for a range of free newsletters and receive exclusive discounts and offers on Packt books and eBooks.

http://PacktLib.PacktPub.com

Do you need instant solutions to your IT questions? PacktLib is Packt's online digital book library. Here, you can access, read and search across Packt's entire library of books.

Why subscribe?

- Fully searchable across every book published by Packt
- Copy and paste, print and bookmark content
- On demand and accessible via web browser

Free access for Packt account holders

If you have an account with Packt at www.PacktPub.com, you can use this to access PacktLib today and view nine entirely free books. Simply use your login credentials for immediate access.

Table of Contents

Preface

As you probably know, the big things in our sphere are those that are moved by the community. Node.js is a technology that has become really popular. Its ecosystem is well-designed and brings with it the flexibility we need. With the rise of mobile development, JavaScript occupies a big part of the technology stack nowadays. The ability to use JavaScript on the server side is really interesting. It's good to know how Node.js works and where and when to use it, but it is more important to see some examples. This book will show you how this wonderful technology handles real use cases.

What this book covers

Chapter 1, *Common Programming Paradigms*, introduces us to the fact that Node.js is a JavaScript-driven technology, and we can apply common design patterns known in JavaScript in Node.js as well.

Chapter 2, *Developing a Basic Site with Node.js and Express*, discusses how ExpressJS is one of the top frameworks on the market. ExpressJS was included because of its fundamental importance in the Node.js world. At the end of the chapter, you will be able to create applications using the built-in Express modules and also add your own modules.

Chapter 3, *Writing a Blog Application with Node.js and AngularJS*, teaches you how to use frontend frameworks such as AngularJS with Node.js. The chapter's example is actually a dynamic application that works with real databases.

Chapter 4, *Developing a Chat with Socket.IO,* explains that nowadays, every big web app uses real-time data. It's important to show instant results to the users. This chapter covers the creation of a simple real-time chat. The same concept can be used to create an automatically updatable HTML component.

Chapter 5, Creating a To-do Application with Backbone.js, illustrates that Backbone.js was one of the first frameworks that introduced data binding at the frontend of applications. This chapter will show you how the library works. The to-do app is a simple example, but perfectly illustrates how powerful the framework is.

Chapter 6, Using Node.js as a Command-line Tool, covers the creation of a simple CLI program. There are a bunch of command-line tools written in Node.js, and the ability to create your own tool is quite satisfying. This part of the book will present a simple application which grabs all the images in a directory and uploads them to Flickr.

Chapter 7, Showing a Social Feed with Ember.js, describes an Ember.js example that will read a Twitter feed and display the latest posts. That's actually a common task of every developer because a lot of applications need to visualize social activity.

Chapter 8, Developing Web App Workflow with Grunt and Gulp, shows that there are a bunch of things to do before you can deliver the application to the users, such as concatenation, minification, templating, and so on. Grunt is the de facto standard for such tasks. The described module optimizes and speeds up your workflow. The chapter presents a simple application setup, including managing JavaScript, CSS, HTML, and cache manifests.

Chapter 9, Automate Your Testing with Node.js, signifies that tests are really important for every application nowadays. Node.js has some really great modules for this. If you are a fan of test-driven development, this chapter is for you.

Chapter 10, Writing Flexible and Modular CSS, introduces the fact that two of the most popular CSS preprocessors are written in Node.js. This chapter is like a little presentation on them and, of course, describes styling a simple web page.

Chapter 11, Writing a REST API, states that Node.js is a fast-working technology, and it is the perfect candidate for building a REST API. You will learn how to create a simple API to store and retrieve data for books, that is, an online library.

Chapter 12, Developing Desktop Apps with Node.js, shows that Node.js is not just a web technology — you can also create desktop apps with it. It's really interesting to know that you can use HTML, CSS, and JavaScript to create desktop programs. Creating a simple file browser may not be such a challenging task, but it will give you enough knowledge to build your own applications.

What you need for this book

You need Node.js installed, a browser, and your favorite code editor. That's all you will use. There are a lot of additional modules to be used, but Node.js comes with a wonderful package manager which handles the installation process.

Who this book is for

The book is for intermediate developers. It teaches you how to use popular Node.js libraries and frameworks. So, good JavaScript knowledge is required.

Conventions

In this book, you will find a number of styles of text that distinguish between different kinds of information. Here are some examples of these styles, and an explanation of their meaning.

Code words in text, database table names, folder names, filenames, file extensions, pathnames, dummy URLs, user input, and Twitter handles are shown as follows: "The `http` module, which we initialize on the first line, is needed for running the web server."

A block of code is set as follows:

```
var http = require('http');
var getTime = function() {
var d = new Date();
return d.getHours() + ':' + d.getMinutes() + ':' +
d.getSeconds() + ':' + d.getMilliseconds();
}
```

Any command-line input or output is written as follows:

```
express --css less myapp
```

New terms and **important words** are shown in bold. Words that you see on the screen, in menus or dialog boxes for example, appear in the text like this: "Click on the blue button with the text **OK, I'LL AUTHORIZE IT**."

> Warnings or important notes appear in a box like this.

> Tips and tricks appear like this.

Reader feedback

Feedback from our readers is always welcome. Let us know what you think about this book—what you liked or may have disliked. Reader feedback is important for us to develop titles that you really get the most out of.

To send us general feedback, simply send an e-mail to feedback@packtpub.com, and mention the book title via the subject of your message.

If there is a topic that you have expertise in and you are interested in either writing or contributing to a book, see our author guide on www.packtpub.com/authors.

Customer support

Now that you are the proud owner of a Packt book, we have a number of things to help you to get the most from your purchase.

Downloading the example code

You can download the example code files for all Packt books you have purchased from your account at http://www.packtpub.com. If you purchased this book elsewhere, you can visit http://www.packtpub.com/support and register to have the files e-mailed directly to you.

Downloading the color images of this book

We also provide you a PDF file that has color images of the screenshots/diagrams used in this book. The color images will help you better understand the changes in the output. You can download this file from: https://www.packtpub.com/sites/default/files/downloads/7338OS_ColoredImages.pdf

Errata

Although we have taken every care to ensure the accuracy of our content, mistakes do happen. If you find a mistake in one of our books — maybe a mistake in the text or the code — we would be grateful if you would report this to us. By doing so, you can save other readers from frustration and help us improve subsequent versions of this book. If you find any errata, please report them by visiting http://www.packtpub.com/submit-errata, selecting your book, clicking on the **errata submission form** link, and entering the details of your errata. Once your errata are verified, your submission will be accepted and the errata will be uploaded on our website, or added to any list of existing errata, under the Errata section of that title. Any existing errata can be viewed by selecting your title from http://www.packtpub.com/support.

Piracy

Piracy of copyright material on the Internet is an ongoing problem across all media. At Packt, we take the protection of our copyright and licenses very seriously. If you come across any illegal copies of our works, in any form, on the Internet, please provide us with the location address or website name immediately so that we can pursue a remedy.

Please contact us at copyright@packtpub.com with a link to the suspected pirated material.

We appreciate your help in protecting our authors, and our ability to bring you valuable content.

Questions

You can contact us at questions@packtpub.com if you are having a problem with any aspect of the book, and we will do our best to address it.

1
Common Programming Paradigms

Node.js is a JavaScript-driven technology. The language has been in development for more than 15 years, and it was first used in Netscape. Over the years, they've found interesting and useful design patterns, which will be of use to us in this book. All this knowledge is now available to Node.js coders. Of course, there are some differences because we are running the code in different environments, but we are still able to apply all these good practices, techniques, and paradigms. I always say that it is important to have a good basis to your applications. No matter how big your application is, it should rely on flexible and well-tested code. The chapter contains proven solutions that guarantee you a good starting point. Knowing design patterns doesn't make you a better developer because in some cases, applying the principles strictly won't work. What you actually get is ideas, which will help you in thinking out of the box. Sometimes, programming is all about managing complexity. We all meet problems, and the key to a well-written application is to find the best suitable solutions. The more paradigms we know, the easier our work is because we have proven concepts that are ready to be applied. That's why this book starts with an introduction to the most common programming paradigms.

Node.js fundamentals

Node.js is a single-threaded technology. This means that every request is processed in only one thread. In other languages, for example, Java, the web server instantiates a new thread for every request. However, Node.js is meant to use asynchronous processing, and there is a theory that doing this in a single thread could bring good performance. The problem of the single-threaded applications is the blocking I/O operations; for example, when we need to read a file from the hard disk to respond to the client. Once a new request lands on our server, we open the file and start reading from it. The problem occurs when another request is generated, and the application is still processing the first one. Let's elucidate the issue with the following example:

```
var http = require('http');
var getTime = function() {
  var d = new Date();
  return  d.getHours() + ':' + d.getMinutes() + ':' +
      d.getSeconds() + ':' + d.getMilliseconds();
}
var respond = function(res, str) {
  res.writeHead(200, {'Content-Type': 'text/plain'});
  res.end(str + '\n');
  console.log(str + ' ' + getTime());
}
var handleRequest = function (req, res) {
  console.log('new request: ' + req.url + ' - ' + getTime());
  if(req.url == '/immediately') {
    respond(res, 'A');
  } else {
    var now = new Date().getTime();
    while(new Date().getTime() < now + 5000) {
      // synchronous reading of the file
    }
    respond(res, 'B');
  }
}
http.createServer(handleRequest).listen(9000, '127.0.0.1');
```

The `http` module, which we initialize on the first line, is needed for running the web server. The `getTime` function returns the current time as a string, and the `respond` function sends a simple text to the browser of the client and reports that the incoming request is processed. The most interesting function is `handleRequest`, which is the entry point of our logic. To simulate the reading of a large file, we will create a `while` cycle for 5 seconds. Once we run the server, we will be able to make an HTTP request to `http://localhost:9000`. In order to demonstrate the single-thread behavior we will send two requests at the same time. These requests are as follows:

- One request will be sent to `http://localhost:9000`, where the server will perform a synchronous operation that takes 5 seconds
- The other request will be sent to `http://localhost:9000/immediately`, where the server should respond immediately

The following screenshot is the output printed from the server, after pinging both the URLs:

```
$ node .\server-test.js
new request: / - 16:58:30:434
B 16:58:35:437
new request: /immediately - 16:58:35:440
A 16:58:35:441
```

As we can see, the first request came at `16:58:30:434`, and its response was sent at `16:58:35:440`, that is, 5 seconds later. However, the problem is that the second request is registered when the first one finishes. That's because the thread belonging to Node.js was busy processing the `while` loop.

Of course, Node.js has a solution for the blocking I/O operations. They are transformed to asynchronous functions that accept callback. Once the operation finishes, Node.js fires the callback, notifying that the job is done. A huge benefit of this approach is that while it waits to get the result of the I/O, the server can process another request. The entity that handles the external events and converts them into callback invocations is called the `event` loop. The `event` loop acts as a really good manager and delegates tasks to various workers. It never blocks and just waits for something to happen; for example, a notification that the file is written successfully.

Now, instead of reading a file synchronously, we will transform our brief example to use asynchronous code. The modified example looks like the following code:

```
var handleRequest = function (req, res) {
  console.log('new request: ' + req.url + ' - ' + getTime());
  if(req.url == '/immediately') {
    respond(res, 'A');
```

```
  } else {
    setTimeout(function() {
      // reading the file
      respond(res, 'B');
      }, 5000);
    }
}
```

The `while` loop is replaced with the `setTimeout` invocation. The result of this change is clearly visible in the server's output, which can be seen in the following screenshot:

```
$ node .\server-test.js
new request: / - 17:54:45:753
new request: /immediately - 17:54:46:82
A 17:54:46:84
B 17:54:50:768
```

The first request still gets its response after 5 seconds. However, the second one is processed immediately.

Organizing your code logic in modules

If we write a lot of code, sooner or later, we will start realizing that our logic should be split into different modules. In most languages, this is done through classes, packages, or some other language-specific syntax. However, in JavaScript, we don't have classes natively. Everything is an object, and in practice, objects inherit other objects. There are several ways to achieve object-oriented programming within JavaScript. You can use prototype inheritance, object literals, or play with function calls. Thankfully, Node.js has a standardized way of defining modules. This is approached by implementing **CommonJS**, which is a project that specifies an ecosystem for JavaScript.

So, you have some logic, and you want to encapsulate it by providing useful API methods. If you reach that moment, you are definitely in the right direction. This is really important, and maybe it is one of the most challenging aspects of programming nowadays. The ability to split our applications into different parts and delegate functions to them is not always an easy task. Very often, this is undervalued, but it's the key to good architecture. If a module contains a lot of dependencies, operates with different data storages, or has several responsibilities, then we are doing something wrong. Such code cannot be tested and is difficult to maintain. Even if we take care about these two things, it is still difficult to extend the code and continue working with it. That's why it's good to define different modules for different functionalities. In the context of Node.js, this is done via the `exports` keyword, which is a reference to `module.exports`.

Building a car construction application

Let's elucidate the process with a simple example. Assume that we are building an application that constructs a car. We need one main module (car) and a few other modules, which are responsible for the different parts of the car (wheels, windows, doors, and so on). Let's start with the definition of a module representing the wheels of the car, with the following code:

```
// wheels.js
var typeOfTires;
exports.init = function(type) {
    typeOfTires = type;
}
exports.info = function() {
  console.log("The car uses " + typeOfTires + " tires.");
}
```

The preceding code could be the content of wheels.js. It contains two methods. The first method, init, should be called first and accepts one setting, that is, the type of the wheels' tires. The second method simply outputs some information. In our main file, car.js, we have to get an instance of the wheels and use the provided API methods. This can be done as follows:

```
// cars.js
  var wheels = require("./wheels.js");
  wheels.init("winter");
  wheels.info();
```

When you run the application with node car.js, you will get the following output:

```
The car uses winter tires.
```

So, everything that you want to expose to the outside world should be attached to the export object. Note that typeOfTires is a local variable for the module. It is available only in wheels.js and not in car.js. It's also a common practice to apply an object or a function to the exports object directly, as shown in the following code for example:

```
// engine.js
var Class = function() {
    // ...
}
Class.prototype = {
  forward: function() {
    console.log("The car is moving forward.");
  },
```

```
      backward: function() {
        console.log("The car is moving backward.");
      }
    }
  }
  module.exports = Class;
```

In JavaScript, everything is an object and that object has a `prototype` property. It's like a storage that keeps the available variables and methods. The `prototype` property is heavily used during inheritance in JavaScript, because it provides a mechanism for transferring logic.

We will also clear the difference between `module.exports` and `exports`. As you can see, in `wheels.js`, we assigned two functions, `init` and `info`, directly to the `exports` global object. In fact, that object is a reference to `module.exports`, and every function or variable attached to it is available to the outside world. However, if we assign a new object or function directly to the `export` object, we should not expect to get an access to it after requiring the file. This should be done with `module.exports`. Let's take the following code as an example:

```
// file.js
module.exports.a = 10;
exports.b = 20;

// app.js
var file = require('./file');
console.log(file.a, file.b);
```

Let's say that both the files, `app.js` and `file.js`, are in the same directory. If we run `node app.js`, we will get `10 20` as the result. However, consider what would happen if we changed the code of `file.js` to the following code:

```
module.exports = { a: 10 };
exports.b = 20;
```

Then, in this case, we would get `10 undefined` as the result. That's because `module.exports` has a new object assigned and `exports` still points to the old one.

Using the car's engine

Let's say that the module in `engine.js` controls the car. It has methods for moving the car forward and backward. It is a little different because the logic is defined in a separate class and that class is directly passed as a value of `module.exports`. In addition, as we are exporting a function, and not just an object, our instance should be created with the `new` keyword. We will see how the car's engine works with the `new` keyword as shown in the following code:

```
var Engine = require("./engine.js");
var e = new Engine();
e.forward();
```

There is a significant difference between using JavaScript functions as constructors and calling them directly. When we call the function as a constructor, we get a new object with its own prototype. If we miss the `new` keyword, the value which we get at the end is the result of the function's invocation.

Node.js caches the modules returned by the `require` method. It's done to prevent the blocking of the `event` loop and increase the performance. It's a synchronous operation, and if there is no cache, Node.js will have to do the same job repeatedly. It's also good to know that we can call the method with just a folder name, but there should be a `package.json` or an `index.js` file inside the directory. All these mechanisms are described well in the official documentation of Node.js at `http://nodejs.org/`. What is important to note here is that the environment encourages modular programming. All we need is native implementation into the system, and we don't have to use a third-party solution that provides modularity.

Like in the client-side code, every Node.js module can be extended. Again, as we are writing the code in plain JavaScript, we can use the well-known approaches for inheritance. For example, take a look at the following code:

```
var Class = function() { }
Class.prototype = new require('./engine.js')();
Class.prototype.constructor = Class;
```

Node.js even offers a helper method for this purpose. Let's say that we want to extend our `engine.js` class and add API methods to move the car in the left and right directions. We can do this with the following piece of code:

```
// control.js
var util = require("util");
var Engine = require("./engine.js");
var Class = function() { }
util.inherits(Class, Engine);
Class.prototype.left = function() {
  console.log("The car is moving to left.");
};
Class.prototype.right = function() {
  console.log("The car is moving to right.");
}
module.exports = Class;
```

The first line gets a reference to the Node.js native `utils` module. It's full of useful functions. The fourth line is where the magic happens. By calling the `inherits` method, we have actually set a new prototype of our `Class` object. Keep in mind that every new method should use the already applied prototype. That's why the `left` and `right` methods are defined after the inheritance. At the end, our car will move in four directions, as shown in the following code snippet:

```
var Control = require("./control.js");
var c = new Control();
c.forward();
c.right();
```

Understanding inter-module communication

We've found out how to put our code logic into modules. Now, we need to know how to make them communicate with each other. Very often, people describe Node.js as an event-driven system. It's also called non-blocking because as we have seen earlier in the chapter, it can accept a new request even before the previous request is fully complete. That's very efficient and highly scalable. The events are very powerful and are good means to inform the other modules of what is going on. They bring about encapsulation, which is very important in modular programming. Let's add some events to the car example we discussed earlier. Let's say that we have air conditioning, and we need to know when it is started. The implementation of such logic consists of two parts. The first one is the air conditioning module. It should dispatch an event that indicates the start of the action. The second part is the other code that listens for that event. We will create a new file called `air.js` containing the logic responsible for the air conditioning, as follows:

```
// air.js
var util = require("util");
var EventEmitter = require('events').EventEmitter;
var Class = function() { }
util.inherits(Class, EventEmitter);
Class.prototype.start = function() {
  this.emit("started");
};
module.exports = Class;
```

Our class extends a Node.js module called `EventEmitter`. It contains methods such as `emit` or `on`, which help us to establish event-based communication. There is only one custom method defined: `start`. It simply dispatches an event that indicates that the air conditioning is turned on. The following code shows how we can attach a listener:

```
// car.js
var AirConditioning = require("./air.js");
var air = new AirConditioning();
air.on("started", function() {
  console.log("Air conditioning started");
});
air.start();
```

A new instance of the `AirConditioning` class is created. We attached an event listener and fired the `start` method. The handler is called, and the message is printed to the console. The example is a simple one but shows how two modules communicate. It's a really powerful approach because it offers encapsulation. The module knows its responsibilities and is not interested in the operations in the other parts of the system. It simply does its job and dispatches notifications (events). For example, in the previous code, the `AirConditioning` class doesn't know that we will output a message when it is started. It only knows that one particular event should be dispatched.

Very often, we need to send data during the emitting of an event. This is really easy. We just have to pass another parameter along with the name of the event. Here is how we send a `status` property:

```
Class.prototype.start = function() {
  this.emit("started", { status: "cold" });
};
```

The object attached to the event contains some information about the air conditioning module. The same object will be available in the listener of the event. The following code shows us how to get the value of the `status` variable mentioned previously:

```
air.on("started", function(data) {
  console.log("Status: " + data.status);
});
```

There is a design pattern that illustrates the preceding process. It's called the **Observer**. In the context of that pattern, our air conditioning module is called **subject**, and the car module is called the observer. The subject broadcasts messages or events to its observers, notifying them that something has changed.

If we need to remove a listener, Node.js has a method for that called
`removeListener`. We can even allow a specific number of observers using
`setMaxListeners`. Overall, the events are one of the best ways to wire your
logical parts. The main benefit is that you isolate the module, but it is still highly
communicative with the rest of your application.

Asynchronous programming

As we already learned, in nonblocking environments, such as Node.js, most of the
processes are asynchronous. A request comes to our code, and our server starts
processing it but at the same time continues to accept new requests. For example,
the following is a simple file reading:

```
fs.readFile('page.html', function (err, content) {
  if (err) throw err;
  console.log(content);
});
```

The `readFile` method accepts two parameters. The first one is a path to the file we
want to read, and the second one is a function that will be called when the operation
finishes. The callback is fired even if the reading fails. Additionally, as everything
can be done via that asynchronous matter, we may end up with a very long callback
chain. There is a term for that—callback hell. To elucidate the problem, we will
extend the previous example and do some operations with the file's content. In the
following code, we are nesting several asynchronous operations:

```
fs.readFile('page.html', function (err, content) {
  if(err) throw err;
  getData(function(data) {
    applyDataToTheTemplate(content, data, function(resultedHTML) {
      renderPage(resultedHTML, function() {
        showPage(function() {
          // finally, we are done
        });
      });
    });
  });
});
```

As you can see, our code looks bad. It's difficult to read and follow. There are a dozen instruments that can help us to avoid such situations. However, we can fix the problem ourselves. The very first step to do is to spot the issue. If we have more than four or five nested callbacks, then we definitely should refactor our code. There is something very simple, which normally helps, that makes the code **shallow**. The previous code could be translated to a more friendly and readable format. For example, see the following code:

```
var onFileRead = function(content) {
  getData(function(data) {
    applyDataToTheTemplate(content, data, dataApplied);
  });
}
var dataApplied = function(resultedHTML) {
  renderPage(resultedHTML, function() {
    showPage(weAreDone);
  });
}
var weAreDone = function() {
  // finally, we are done
}
fs.readFile('page.html', function (err, content) {
  if (err) throw err;
    onFileRead(content);
});
```

Most of the callbacks are just defined separately. It is clear what is going on because the functions have descriptive names. However, in more complex situations, this technique may not work because you will need to define a lot of methods. If that's the case, then it is good to combine the functions in an external module. The previous example can be transformed to a module that accepts the name of a file and the callback function. The module is as follows:

```
var renderTemplate = require("./renderTemplate.js");
renderTemplate('page.html', function() {
  // we are done
});
```

You still have a callback, but it looks like the helper methods are hidden and only the main functionality is visible.

Another popular instrument for dealing with asynchronous code is the **promises** paradigm. We already talked about events in JavaScript, and the promises are something similar to them. We are still waiting for something to happen and pass a callback. We can say that the promises represent a value that is not available at the moment but will be available in the future. The syntax of promises makes the asynchronous code look synchronous. Let's see an example where we have a simple module that loads a Twitter feed. The example is as follows:

```
var TwitterFeed = require('TwitterFeed');
TwitterFeed.on('loaded', function(err, data) {
  if(err) {
      // ...
    } else {
      // ...
    }
});
TwitterFeed.getData();
```

We attached a listener for the `loaded` event and called the `getData` method, which connects to Twitter and fetches the information. The following code is what the same example will look like if the `TwitterFeed` class supports promises:

```
var TwitterFeed = require('TwitterFeed');
var promise = TwitterFeed.getData();
promise.then(function(data) {
  // ...
}, function(err) {
  // ...
});
```

The `promise` object represents our data. The first function, which is sent to the `then` method, is called when the `promise` object succeeds. Note that the callbacks are registered after calling the `getData` method. This means that we are not rigid to actual process of getting the data. We are not interested in when the action occurs. We only care when it finishes and what its result is. We can spot a few differences from the event-based implementation. They are as follows:

- There is a separate function for error handling.
- The `getData` method can be called before calling the `then` method. However, the same thing is not possible with events. We need to attach the listeners before running the logic. Otherwise, if our task is synchronous, the event may be dispatched before our listener attachment.
- The **promise** method can only succeed or fail once, while one specific event may be fired multiple times and its handlers can be called multiple times.

The promises get really handy when we chain them. To elucidate this, we will use the same example and save the tweets to a database with the following code:

```
var TwitterFeed = require('TwitterFeed');
var Database = require('Database');
var promise = TwitterFeed.getData();
promise.then(function(data) {
  var promise = Database.save(data);
  return promise;
}).then(function() {
  // the data is saved
  // into the database
}).catch(function(err) {
  // ...
});
```

So, if our successful callback returns a new promise, we can use `then` for the second time. Also, we have the possibility to set only one error handler. The `catch` method at the end is fired if some of the promises are rejected.

There are four states of every promise, and we should mention them here because it's a terminology that is widely used. A promise could be in any of the following states:

- **Fulfilled**: A promise is in the fulfilled state when the action related to the promise succeeds
- **Rejected**: A promise is in the rejected state when the action related to the promise fails
- **Pending**: A promise is in the pending state if it hasn't been fulfilled or rejected yet
- **Settled**: A promise is in a settled state when it has been fulfilled or rejected

The asynchronous nature of JavaScript makes our coding really interesting. However, it could sometimes lead to a lot of problems. Here is a wrap up of the discussed ideas to deal with the issues:

- Try to use more functions instead of closures
- Avoid the pyramid-looking code by removing the closures and defining top-level functions
- Use events
- Use promises

Exploring middleware architecture

The Node.js framework is based on the middleware architecture. That's because this architecture brings modularity. It's really easy to add or remove functionalities from the system without breaking the application because the different modules do not depend on each other. Imagine that we have several modules that are all stored in an array, and our application starts using them one by one. We are controlling the whole process, that is, the execution continues only if we want it to. The concept is demonstrated in the following diagram:

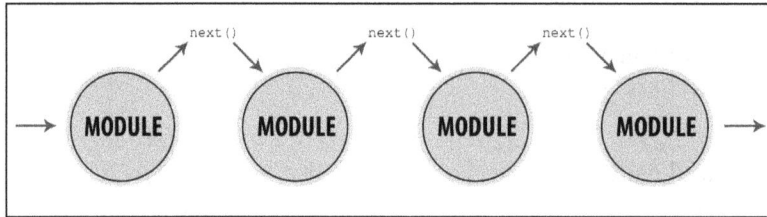

Connect (`https://github.com/senchalabs/connect`) is one of the first frameworks that implements this pattern. In the context of Node.js, the middleware is a function that accepts the request, response, and the next callbacks. The first two parameters represent the input and output of the middleware. The last one is a way to pass the flow to the next middleware in the list. The following is a short example of this:

```
var connect = require('connect'),
    http = require('http');

var app = connect()
  .use(function(req, res, next) {
    console.log("That's my first middleware");
    next();
  })
  .use(function(req, res, next) {
    console.log("That's my second middleware");
    next();
  })
  .use(function(req, res, next) {
    console.log("end");
    res.end("hello world");
  });

http.createServer(app).listen(3000);
```

The use method of connect accepts middleware. In general, the middleware is just a simple JavaScript function. We can write whatever we want in it. What is important to do at the end is to call the next method. It passes the flow to the next middleware. Often, we will need to transfer data between the middleware. It's a common practice to modify the request or the response objects because they are the input and output of the module. We can attach new properties or functions, and they will be available for the next middleware in the list. As in the following code snippet, we are attaching an object to a data property.

```
.use(function(req, res, next) {
    req.data = { value: "middleware"};
    next();
})
.use(function(req, res, next) {
    console.log(req.data.value);
})
```

The request and response objects are identical in every function. Thus, the middleware share the same scope. At the same time, they are completely independent. This pattern provides a really flexible development environment. We can combine modules that do different tasks written by different developers.

Composition versus inheritance

In the previous section, we learned how to create modules, how to make them communicate, and how to use them. Let's talk a bit about how to architect modules. There are dozens of ways to build a good application. There are also some great books written only on this subject, but we will focus on two of the most commonly used techniques: composition and inheritance. It's really important to understand the difference between the two. They both have pros and cons. In most of the cases, their usage depends on the current project.

The car class from the previous sections is a perfect example of composition. The functionalities of the car object are built by other small objects. So, the main module actually delegates its jobs to other classes. For example, the wheels or the air conditioning of the car are controlled by externally defined modules:

```
var wheels = require("./wheels.js")();
var control = require("./control.js")();
var airConditioning = require("./air.js")();
module.export = {
  run: function() {
    wheels.init();
```

```
        control.forward();
        airConditioning.start();
    }
}
```

For the outside world, the car has only one method: run. However, what happens is that we perform three different operations, and they are defined in other modules. Often, the composition is preferred over the inheritance because while using this approach, we can easily add as many modules as we want. It's also interesting that we cannot only include modules but also other compositions.

On the other side is the inheritance. The following code is a typical example of inheritance:

```
var util = require("util");
var EventEmitter = require('events').EventEmitter;
var Class = function() { }
util.inherits(Class, EventEmitter);
```

This code implies that our class needs to be an event emitter, so it simply inherits that functionality from another class. Of course, in this case, we can still use composition and create an instance of the EventEmitter class, define methods such as on and dispatch, and delegate the real work. However, here it is much better to use inheritance.

The truth is somewhere in between—the composition and the inheritance should play together. They are really great tools, but each of them has its own place. It's not only black and white, and sometimes it is difficult to find the right direction. There are three ways to add behavior to our objects. They are as follows:

- Writing the functionality into the objects directly
- Inheriting the functionality from a class that already has the desired behavior
- Creating a local instance of an object that does the job

The second one is related to inheritance and the last one is actually a composition. By using composition, we are adding a few more abstraction layers, which is not a bad thing, but it could lead to unnecessary complexity.

Managing dependencies

Dependency management is one of the biggest problems in complex software. Often, we build our applications around third-party libraries or custom-made modules written for other projects. We do this because we don't want to reinvent the wheel every time.

In the previous sections of this chapter, we used the `require` global function. That's how Node.js adds dependencies to the current module. A functionality written in one JavaScript file is included in another file. The good thing is that the logic in the imported file lives in its own scope, and only the publicly exported functions and variables are visible to the host. With this behavior, we are able to separate our logic modules into Node.js packages. There is an instrument that controls such packages. It's called **Node Package Manager** (**npm**) and is available as a command-line instrument. Node.js has become so popular mainly because of the existence of its package manager. Every developer can publish their own package and share it with the community. The good versioning helps us to bind our applications to specific versions of the dependencies, which means that we can use a module that depends on other modules. The main rule to make this work is to add a `package.json` file to our project. We will add this file with the following code:

```json
{
  "name": "my-awesome-module",
  "version": "0.1.10",
  "dependencies": {
    "optimist": "0.6.1",
    "colors": "0.6.2"
  }
}
```

The content of the file should be valid JSON and should contain at least the `name` and `version` fields. The `name` property should also be unique, and there should not be any other module with the same name. The `dependencies` property contains all the modules and versions that we depend on. To the same file, we can add a lot of other properties. For example, information about the author, a description of the package, the license of the project, or even keywords. Once the module is registered in the registry, we can use it as a dependency. We just need to add it in our `package.json` file, and after we run `npm install`, we will be able to use it as a dependency. Since Node.js adopts the module pattern, we don't need instruments such as the dependency injection container or service locater.

Let's write a `package.json` file for the car example used in the previous sections, as follows:

```json
{
  "name": "my-awesome-car",
  "version": "0.0.1",
  "dependencies": {
    "wheels": "2.0.1",
    "control": "0.1.2",
    "air": "0.2.4"
  }
}
```

Summary

In this chapter, we went through the most common programming paradigms in Node.js. We learned how Node.js handles parallel requests. We understood how to write modules and make them communicative. We saw the problems of the asynchronous code and their most popular solutions. At the end of the chapter, we talked about how to construct our application. With all this as a basis, we can start thinking about better programs. Software writing is not an easy task and requires strong knowledge and experience. The experience usually comes after years of coding; however, knowledge is something that we can get instantly. Node.js is a young technology; nonetheless, we are able to apply paradigms and concepts from client-side JavaScript and even other languages.

In the next chapter, we will see how to use one of the most popular frameworks for Node.js, that is, Express.js, and we will build a simple website.

2
Developing a Basic Site with Node.js and Express

In the previous chapter, we learned about common programming paradigms and how they apply to Node.js. In this chapter, we will continue with the **Express** framework. It's one of the most popular frameworks available and is certainly a pioneering one. Express is still widely used and several developers use it as a starting point.

Getting acquainted with Express

Express (http://expressjs.com/) is a web application framework for Node.js. It is built on top of Connect (http://www.senchalabs.org/connect/), which means that it implements middleware architecture. In the previous chapter, when exploring Node.js, we discovered the benefit of such a design decision: the framework acts as a plugin system. Thus, we can say that Express is suitable for not only simple but also complex applications because of its architecture. We may use only some of the popular types of middleware or add a lot of features and still keep the application modular.

In general, most projects in Node.js perform two functions: run a server that listens on a specific port, and process incoming requests. Express is a wrapper for these two functionalities. The following is basic code that runs the server:

```
var http = require('http');
http.createServer(function (req, res) {
  res.writeHead(200, {'Content-Type': 'text/plain'});
  res.end('Hello World\n');
}).listen(1337, '127.0.0.1');
console.log('Server running at http://127.0.0.1:1337/');
```

This is an example extracted from the official documentation of Node.js. As shown, we use the native module `http` and run a server on the port `1337`. There is also a request handler function, which simply sends the `Hello world` string to the browser. Now, let's implement the same thing but with the Express framework, using the following code:

```
var express = require('express');
var app = express();
app.get("/", function(req, res, next) {
  res.send("Hello world");
}).listen(1337);
console.log('Server running at http://127.0.0.1:1337/');
```

It's pretty much the same thing. However, we don't need to specify the response headers or add a new line at the end of the string because the framework does it for us. In addition, we have a bunch of middleware available, which will help us process the requests easily. Express is like a toolbox. We have a lot of tools to do the boring stuff, allowing us to focus on the application's logic and content. That's what Express is built for: saving time for the developer by providing ready-to-use functionalities.

Installing Express

There are two ways to install Express. We'll will start with the simple one and then proceed to the more advanced technique. The simpler approach generates a template, which we may use to start writing the business logic directly. In some cases, this can save us time. From another viewpoint, if we are developing a custom application, we need to use custom settings. We can also use the boilerplate, which we get with the advanced technique; however, it may not work for us.

Using package.json

Express is like every other module. It has its own place in the packages register. If we want to use it, we need to add the framework in the `package.json` file. The ecosystem of Node.js is built on top of the Node Package Manager. It uses the JSON file to find out what we need and installs it in the current directory. So, the content of our `package.json` file looks like the following code:

```
{
  "name": "projectname",
  "description": "description",
  "version": "0.0.1",
  "dependencies": {
```

```
      "express": "3.x"
  }
}
```

These are the required fields that we have to add. To be more accurate, we have to say that the mandatory fields are `name` and `version`. However, it is always good to add descriptions to our modules, particularly if we want to publish our work in the registry, where such information is extremely important. Otherwise, the other developers will not know what our library is doing. Of course, there are a bunch of other fields, such as contributors, keywords, or development dependencies, but we will stick to limited options so that we can focus on Express.

Once we have our `package.json` file placed in the project's folder, we have to call `npm install` in the console. By doing so, the package manager will create a `node_modules` folder and will store Express and its dependencies there. At the end of the command's execution, we will see something like the following screenshot:

```
express@4.0.0 node_modules\express
├── methods@0.1.0
├── parseurl@1.0.1
├── merge-descriptors@0.0.2
├── utils-merge@1.0.0
├── escape-html@1.0.1
├── debug@0.8.0
├── cookie-signature@1.0.3
├── range-parser@1.0.0
├── fresh@0.2.2
├── qs@0.6.6
├── buffer-crc32@0.2.1
├── cookie@0.1.0
├── path-to-regexp@0.1.2
├── type-is@1.0.0 (mime@1.2.11)
├── send@0.2.0 (mime@1.2.11)
├── accepts@1.0.0 (mime@1.2.11, negotiator@0.3.0)
└── serve-static@1.0.1 (send@0.1.4)
```

The first line shows us the installed version, and the proceeding lines are actually modules that Express depends on. Now, we are ready to use Express. If we type `require('express')`, Node.js will start looking for that library inside the local `node_modules` directory. Since we are not using absolute paths, this is normal behavior. If we miss running the `npm install` command, we will be prompted with `Error: Cannot find module 'express'`.

Using a command-line tool

There is a command-line instrument called `express-generator`. Once we run `npm install -g express-generator`, we will install and use it as every other command in our terminal.

If you use the framework in several projects, you will notice that some things are repeated. We can even copy and paste them from one application to another, and this is perfectly fine. We may even end up with our own boilerplate and can always start from there. The command-line version of Express does the same thing. It accepts few arguments and based on them, creates a skeleton for use. This can be very handy in some cases and will definitely save some time. Let's have a look at the available arguments:

- `-h, --help`: This signifies output usage information.
- `-V, --version`: This shows the version of Express.
- `-e, --ejs`: This argument adds the EJS template engine support. Normally, we need a library to deal with our templates. Writing pure HTML is not very practical. The default engine is set to JADE.
- `-H, --hogan`: This argument is Hogan-enabled (another template engine).
- `-c, --css`: If we want to use the CSS preprocessors, this option lets us use **LESS** (short for **Leaner CSS**) or Stylus. The default is plain CSS.
- `-f, --force`: This forces Express to operate on a nonempty directory.

Let's try to generate an Express application skeleton with LESS as a CSS preprocessor. We use the following line of command:

```
express --css less myapp
```

A new `myapp` folder is created with the file structure, as seen in the following screenshot:

```
└─ myapp
    └─ bin
        └─ www
    └─ public
        └─ images
        └─ javascripts
        └─ stylesheets
    └─ routes
        └─ index.js
        └─ user.js
    └─ views
        └─ error.jade
        └─ index.jade
        └─ layout.jade
    └─ app.js
    └─ package.json
```

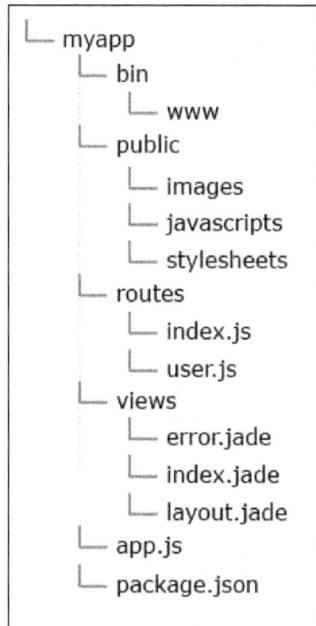

We still need to install the dependencies, so `cd myapp && npm install` is required. We will skip the explanation of the generated directories for now and will move to the created `app.js` file. It starts with initializing the module dependencies, as follows:

```
var express = require('express');
var path = require('path');
var favicon = require('static-favicon');
var logger = require('morgan');
var cookieParser = require('cookie-parser');
var bodyParser = require('body-parser');

var routes = require('./routes/index');
var users = require('./routes/users');

var app = express();
```

Our framework is `express`, and `path` is a native Node.js module. The middleware are `favicon`, `logger`, `cookieParser`, and `bodyParser`. The `routes` and `users` are custom-made modules, placed in local for the project folders. Similarly, as in the **Model-View-Controller (MVC)** pattern, these are the controllers for our application. Immediately after, an `app` variable is created; this represents the Express library. We use this variable to configure our application. The script continues by setting some key-value pairs. The next code snippet defines the path to our views and the default template engine:

```
app.set('views', path.join(__dirname, 'views'));
app.set('view engine', 'jade');
```

The framework uses the methods `set` and `get` to define the internal properties. In fact, we may use these methods to define our own variables. If the value is a Boolean, we can replace `set` and `get` with `enable` and `disable`. For example, see the following code:

```
app.set('color', 'red');
app.get('color'); // red
app.enable('isAvailable');
```

The next code adds middleware to the framework. We can see the code as follows:

```
app.use(favicon());
app.use(logger('dev'));
app.use(bodyParser.json());
app.use(bodyParser.urlencoded());
app.use(cookieParser());
app.use(require('less-middleware')({ src: path.join(__dirname,
'public') }));
app.use(express.static(path.join(__dirname, 'public')));
```

The first middleware serves as the favicon of our application. The second is responsible for the output in the console. If we remove it, we will not get information about the incoming requests to our server. The following is a simple output produced by `logger`:

```
GET / 200 554ms - 170b
GET /stylesheets/style.css 200 18ms - 110b
```

The json and urlencoded middleware are related to the data sent along with the request. We need them because they convert the information in an easy-to-use format. There is also a middleware for the cookies. It populates the request object, so we later have access to the required data. The generated app uses LESS as a CSS preprocessor, and we need to configure it by setting the directory containing the .less files. We will talk about LESS in *Chapter 10, Writing Flexible and Modular CSS,* where will cover this in detail. Eventually, we define our static resources, which should be delivered by the server. These are just few lines, but we've configured the whole application. We may remove or replace some of the modules, and the others will continue working. The next code in the file maps two defined routes to two different handlers, as follows:

```
app.use('/', routes);
app.use('/users', users);
```

If the user tries to open a missing page, Express still processes the request by forwarding it to the error handler, as follows:

```
app.use(function(req, res, next) {
    var err = new Error('Not Found');
    err.status = 404;
    next(err);
});
```

The framework suggests two types of error handling: one for the development environment and another for the production server. The difference is that the second one hides the stack trace of the error, which should be visible only for the developers of the application. As we can see in the following code, we are checking the value of the env property and handling the error differently:

```
// development error handler
if (app.get('env') === 'development') {
    app.use(function(err, req, res, next) {
        res.status(err.status || 500);
        res.render('error', {
            message: err.message,
            error: err
        });
    });
}
// production error handler
app.use(function(err, req, res, next) {
    res.status(err.status || 500);
```

```
        res.render('error', {
            message: err.message,
            error: {}
        });
    });
```

At the end, the `app.js` file exports the created Express instance, as follows:

```
module.exports = app;
```

To run the application, we need to execute `node ./bin/www`. The code requires `app.js` and starts the server, which by default listens on port `3000`.

```
#!/usr/bin/env node
var debug = require('debug')('my-application');
var app = require('../app');

app.set('port', process.env.PORT || 3000);

var server = app.listen(app.get('port'), function() {
  debug('Express server listening on port ' + server.address().port);
});
```

The `process.env` declaration provides an access to variables defined in the current development environment. If there is no `PORT` setting, Express uses 3000 as the value. The required `debug` module uses a similar approach to find out whether it has to show messages to the console.

Managing routes

The input of our application is the routes. The user visits our page at a specific URL and we have to map this URL to a specific logic. In the context of Express, this can be done easily, as follows:

```
var controller = function(req, res, next) {
  res.send("response");
}
app.get('/example/url', controller);
```

We even have control over the HTTP's method, that is, we are able to catch POST, PUT, or DELETE requests. This is very handy if we want to retain the address path but apply a different logic. For example, see the following code:

```
var getUsers = function(req, res, next) {
  // ...
}
```

```
var createUser = function(req, res, next) {
  // ...
}
app.get('/users', getUsers);
app.post('/users', createUser);
```

The path is still the same, /users, but if we make a POST request to that URL, the application will try to create a new user. Otherwise, if the method is GET, it will return a list of all the registered members. There is also a method, app.all, which we can use to handle all the method types at once. We can see this method in the following code snippet:

```
app.all('/', serverHomePage);
```

There is something interesting about the routing in Express. We may pass not just one but many handlers. This means that we can create a chain of functions that correspond to one URL. For example, it we need to know if the user is logged in, there is a module for that. We can add another method that validates the current user and attaches a variable to the request object, as follows:

```
var isUserLogged = function(req, res, next) {
  req.userLogged = Validator.isCurrentUserLogged();
  next();
}
var getUser = function(req, res, next) {
  if(req.userLogged) {
    res.send("You are logged in. Hello!");
  } else {
    res.send("Please log in first.");
  }
}
app.get('/user', isUserLogged, getUser);
```

The Validator class is a class that checks the current user's session. The idea is simple: we add another handler, which acts as an additional middleware. After performing the necessary actions, we call the next function, which passes the flow to the next handler, getUser. Because the request and response objects are the same for all the middlewares, we have access to the userLogged variable. This is what makes Express really flexible. There are a lot of great features available, but they are optional. At the end of this chapter, we will make a simple website that implements the same logic.

Handling dynamic URLs and the HTML forms

The Express framework also supports dynamic URLs. Let's say we have a separate page for every user in our system. The address to those pages looks like the following code:

```
/user/45/profile
```

Here, 45 is the unique number of the user in our database. It's of course normal to use one route handler for this functionality. We can't really define different functions for every user. The problem can be solved by using the following syntax:

```
var getUser = function(req, res, next) {
  res.send("Show user with id = " + req.params.id);
}
app.get('/user/:id/profile', getUser);
```

The route is actually like a regular expression with variables inside. Later, that variable is accessible in the `req.params` object. We can have more than one variable. Here is a slightly more complex example:

```
var getUser = function(req, res, next) {
  var userId = req.params.id;
  var actionToPerform = req.params.action;
  res.send("User (" + userId + "): " + actionToPerform)
}
app.get('/user/:id/profile/:action', getUser);
```

If we open `http://localhost:3000/user/451/profile/edit`, we see `User (451): edit` as a response. This is how we can get a nice looking, SEO-friendly URL.

Of course, sometimes we need to pass data via the GET or POST parameters. We may have a request like `http://localhost:3000/user?action=edit`. To parse it easily, we need to use the native `url` module, which has few helper functions to parse URLs:

```
var getUser = function(req, res, next) {
  var url = require('url');
  var url_parts = url.parse(req.url, true);
  var query = url_parts.query;
  res.send("User: " + query.action);
}
app.get('/user', getUser);
```

Once the module parses the given URL, our GET parameters are stored in the `.query` object. The POST variables are a bit different. We need a new middleware to handle that. Thankfully, Express has one, which is as follows:

```
app.use(express.bodyParser());
var getUser = function(req, res, next) {
  res.send("User: " + req.body.action);
}
app.post('/user', getUser);
```

The `express.bodyParser()` middleware populates the `req.body` object with the POST data. Of course, we have to change the HTTP method from `.get` to `.post` or `.all`.

If we want to read cookies in Express, we may use the `cookieParser` middleware. Similar to the body parser, it should also be installed and added to the `package.json` file. The following example sets the middleware and demonstrates its usage:

```
var cookieParser = require('cookie-parser');
app.use(cookieParser('optional secret string'));
app.get('/', function(req, res, next){
    var prop = req.cookies.propName
});
```

Returning a response

Our server accepts requests, does some stuff, and finally, sends the response to the client's browser. This can be HTML, JSON, XML, or binary data, among others. As we know, by default, every middleware in Express accepts two objects, `request` and `response`. The `response` object has methods that we can use to send an answer to the client. Every response should have a proper content type or length. Express simplifies the process by providing functions to set HTTP headers and sending content to the browser. In most cases, we will use the `.send` method, as follows:

```
res.send("simple text");
```

When we pass a string, the framework sets the `Content-Type` header to `text/html`. It's great to know that if we pass an object or array, the content type is `application/json`. If we develop an API, the response status code is probably going to be important for us. With Express, we are able to set it like in the following code snippet:

```
res.send(404, 'Sorry, we cannot find that!');
```

It's even possible to respond with a file from our hard disk. If we don't use the framework, we will need to read the file, set the correct HTTP headers, and send the content. However, Express offers the .sendfile method, which wraps all these operations as follows:

```
res.sendfile(__dirname + "/images/photo.jpg");
```

Again, the content type is set automatically; this time it is based on the filename's extension.

When building websites or applications with a user interface, we normally need to serve an HTML. Sure, we can write it manually in JavaScript, but it's good practice to use a template engine. This means we save everything in external files and the engine reads the markup from there. It populates them with some data and, at the end, provides ready-to-show content. In Express, the whole process is summarized in one method, .render. However, to work properly, we have to instruct the framework regarding which template engine to use. We already talked about this in the beginning of this chapter. The following two lines of code, set the path to our views and the template engine:

```
app.set('views', path.join(__dirname, 'views'));
app.set('view engine', 'jade');
```

Let's say we have the following template (/views/index.jade):

```
h1= title
p Welcome to #{title}
```

Express provides a method to serve templates. It accepts the path to the template, the data to be applied, and a callback. To render the previous template, we should use the following code:

```
res.render("index", {title: "Page title here"});
```

The HTML produced looks as follows:

```
<h1>Page title here</h1><p>Welcome to Page title here</p>
```

If we pass a third parameter, function, we will have access to the generated HTML. However, it will not be sent as a response to the browser.

The example-logging system

We've seen the main features of Express. Now let's build something real. The next few pages present a simple website where users can read only if they are logged in. Let's start and set up the application. We are going to use Express' command-line instrument. It should be installed using `npm install -g express-generator`. We create a new folder for the example, navigate to it via the terminal, and execute `express --css less site`. A new directory, `site`, will be created. If we go there and run `npm install`, Express will download all the required dependencies. As we saw earlier, by default, we have two routes and two controllers. To simplify the example, we will use only the first one: `app.use('/', routes)`. Let's change the `views/index.jade` file content to the following HTML code:

```
doctype html
html
  head
    title= title
    link(rel='stylesheet', href='/stylesheets/style.css')
  body
    h1= title
    hr
    p That's a simple application using Express.
```

Now, if we run `node ./bin/www` and open `http://127.0.0.1:3000`, we will see the page. Jade uses indentation to parse our template. So, we should not mix tabs and spaces. Otherwise, we will get an error.

Next, we need to protect our content. We check whether the current user has a session created; if not, a login form is shown. It's the perfect time to create a new middleware.

To use sessions in Express, install an additional module: `express-session`. We need to open our `package.json` file and add the following line of code:

```
"express-session": "~1.0.0"
```

Once we do that, a quick run of `npm install` will bring the module to our application. All we have to do is use it. The following code goes to `app.js`:

```
var session = require('express-session');
app.use(session({ secret: 'app', cookie: { maxAge: 60000 }}));
var verifyUser = function(req, res, next) {
    if(req.session.loggedIn) {
```

```
        next();
    } else {
        res.send("show login form");
    }
}
app.use('/', verifyUser, routes);
```

Note that we changed the original `app.use('/', routes)` line. The `session` middleware is initialized and added to Express. The `verifyUser` function is called before the page rendering. It uses the `req.session` object, and checks whether there is a `loggedIn` variable defined and if its value is `true`. If we run the script again, we will see that the `show login form` text is shown for every request. It's like this because no code sets the session exactly the way we want it. We need a form where users can type their username and password. We will process the result of the form and if the credentials are correct, the `loggedIn` variable will be set to `true`. Let's create a new `Jade` template, `/views/login.jade`:

```
doctype html
html
  head
    title= title
    link(rel='stylesheet', href='/stylesheets/style.css')
  body
    h1= title
    hr
    form(method='post')
      label Username:
      br
      input(type='text', name='username')
      br
      label Password:
      br
      input(type='password', name='password')
      br
      input(type='submit')
```

Instead of sending just a text with `res.send("show login form");` we should render the new template, as follows:

```
res.render("login", {title: "Please log in."});
```

We choose POST as the method for the form. So, we need to add the middleware that populates the `req.body` object with the user's data, as follows:

```
app.use(bodyParser());
```

Process the submitted username and password as follows:

```
var verifyUser = function(req, res, next) {
  if(req.session.loggedIn) {
    next();
  } else {
    var username = "admin", password = "admin";
    if(req.body.username === username &&
    req.body.password === password) {
      req.session.loggedIn = true;
      res.redirect('/');
    } else {
      res.render("login", {title: "Please log in."});
    }
  }
}
```

The valid credentials are set to admin/admin. In a real application, we may need to access a database or get this information from another place. It's not really a good idea to place the username and password in the code; however, for our little experiment, it is fine. The previous code checks whether the passed data matches our predefined values. If everything is correct, it sets the session, after which the user is forwarded to the home page.

Once you log in, you should be able to log out. Let's add a link for that just after the content on the index page (views/index.jade):

```
a(href='/logout') logout
```

Once users clicks on this link, they will be forward to a new page. We just need to create a handler for the new route, remove the session, and forward them to the index page where the login form is reflected. Here is what our logging out handler looks like:

```
// in app.js
var logout = function(req, res, next) {
  req.session.loggedIn = false;
  res.redirect('/');
}
app.all('/logout', logout);
```

Setting loggedIn to false is enough to make the session invalid. The redirect sends users to the same content page they came from. However, this time, the content is hidden and the login form pops up.

Summary

In this chapter, we learned about one of most widely used Node.js frameworks, Express. We discussed its fundamentals, how to set it up, and its main characteristics. The middleware architecture, which we mentioned in the previous chapter, is the base of the library and gives us the power to write complex but, at the same time, flexible applications. The example we used was a simple one. We required a valid session to provide page access. However, it illustrates the usage of the body parser middleware and the process of registering the new routes. We also updated the Jade templates and saw the results in the browser.

The next chapter will show us how Node.js collaborated with AngularJS, a popular framework made by Google for client-side JavaScript applications.

3
Writing a Blog Application with Node.js and AngularJS

In this chapter, we are going to build a blog application by using Node.js and AngularJS. Our system will support adding, editing, and removing articles, so there will be a control panel. The MongoDB or MySQL database will handle the storing of the information and the Express framework will be used as the site base. It will deliver the JavaScript, CSS, and the HTML to the end user, and will provide an API to access the database. We will use AngularJS to build the user interface and control the client-side logic in the administration page.

This chapter will cover the following topics:

- AngularJS fundamentals
- Choosing and initializing a database
- Implementing the client-side part of an application with AngularJS

Exploring AngularJS

AngularJS is an open source, client-side JavaScript framework developed by Google. It's full of features and is really well documented. It has almost become a standard framework in the development of single-page applications. The official site of AngularJS, http://angularjs.org, provides a well-structured documentation. As the framework is widely used, there is a lot of material in the form of articles and video tutorials. As a JavaScript library, it collaborates pretty well with Node.js. In this chapter, we will build a simple blog with a control panel.

Before we start developing our application, let's first take a look at the framework. AngularJS gives us very good control over the data on our page. We don't have to think about selecting elements from the DOM and filling them with values. Thankfully, due to the available data-binding, we may update the data in the JavaScript part and see the change in the HTML part. This is also true for the reverse. Once we change something in the HTML part, we get the new values in the JavaScript part. The framework has a powerful dependency injector. There are predefined classes in order to perform AJAX requests and manage routes.

You could also read *Mastering Web Development with AngularJS* by Peter Bacon Darwin and Pawel Kozlowski, published by Packt Publishing.

Bootstrapping AngularJS applications

To bootstrap an AngularJS application, we need to add the `ng-app` attribute to some of our HTML tags. It is important that we pick the right one. Having `ng-app` somewhere means that all the child nodes will be processed by the framework. It's common practice to put that attribute on the `<html>` tag. In the following code, we have a simple HTML page containing ng-app:

```
<html ng-app>
    <head>
        <script src="angular.min.js"></script>
    </head>
    <body>
        ...
    </body>
</html>
```

Very often, we will apply a value to the attribute. This will be a module name. We will do this while developing the control panel of our blog application. Having the freedom to place `ng-app` wherever we want means that we can decide which part of our markup will be controlled by AngularJS. That's good, because if we have a giant HTML file, we really don't want to spend resources parsing the whole document. Of course, we may bootstrap our logic manually, and this is needed when we have more than one AngularJS application on the page.

Using directives and controllers

In AngularJS, we can implement the Model-View-Controller pattern. The controller acts as glue between the data (model) and the user interface (view). In the context of the framework, the controller is just a simple function. For example, the following HTML code illustrates that a controller is just a simple function:

```
<html ng-app>
    <head>
```

```
        <script src="angular.min.js"></script>
        <script src="HeaderController.js"></script>
    </head>
    <body>
        <header ng-controller="HeaderController">
            <h1>{{title}}</h1>
        </header>
    </body>
</html>
```

In `<head>` of the page, we are adding the minified version of the library and `HeaderController.js`; a file that will host the code of our controller. We also set an `ng-controller` attribute in the HTML markup. The definition of the controller is as follows:

```
function HeaderController($scope) {
    $scope.title = "Hello world";
}
```

Every controller has its own area of influence. That area is called the scope. In our case, `HeaderController` defines the `{{title}}` variable. AngularJS has a wonderful dependency-injection system. Thankfully, due to this mechanism, the `$scope` argument is automatically initialized and passed to our function. The `ng-controller` attribute is called the directive, that is, an attribute, which has meaning to AngularJS. There are a lot of directives that we can use. That's maybe one of the strongest points of the framework. We can implement complex logic directly inside our templates, for example, data binding, filtering, or modularity.

Data binding

Data binding is a process of automatically updating the view once the model is changed. As we mentioned earlier, we can change a variable in the JavaScript part of the application and the HTML part will be automatically updated. We don't have to create a reference to a DOM element or attach event listeners. Everything is handled by the framework. Let's continue and elaborate on the previous example, as follows:

```
<header ng-controller="HeaderController">
  <h1>{{title}}</h1>
  <a href="#" ng-click="updateTitle()">change title</a>
</header>
```

A link is added and it contains the `ng-click` directive. The `updateTitle` function is a function defined in the controller, as seen in the following code snippet:

```
function HeaderController($scope) {
  $scope.title = "Hello world";
```

```
    $scope.updateTitle = function() {
      $scope.title = "That's a new title.";
    }
  }
}
```

We don't care about the DOM element and where the {{title}} variable is. We just change a property of $scope and everything works. There are, of course, situations where we will have the <input> fields and we want to bind their values. If that's the case, then the ng-model directive can be used. We can see this as follows:

```
<header ng-controller="HeaderController">
  <h1>{{title}}</h1>
  <a href="#" ng-click="updateTitle()">change title</a>
  <input type="text" ng-model="title" />
</header>
```

The data in the input field is bound to the same title variable. This time, we don't have to edit the controller. AngularJS automatically changes the content of the h1 tag.

Encapsulating logic with modules

It's great that we have controllers. However, it's not a good practice to place everything into globally defined functions. That's why it is good to use the module system. The following code shows how a module is defined:

```
angular.module('HeaderModule', []);
```

The first parameter is the name of the module and the second one is an array with the module's dependencies. By dependencies, we mean other modules, services, or something custom that we can use inside the module. It should also be set as a value of the ng-app directive. The code so far could be translated to the following code snippet:

```
angular.module('HeaderModule', [])
.controller('HeaderController', function($scope) {
  $scope.title = "Hello world";
  $scope.updateTitle = function() {
    $scope.title = "That's a new title.";
  }
});
```

So, the first line defines a module. We can chain the different methods of the module and one of them is the controller method. Following this approach, that is, putting our code inside a module, we will be encapsulating logic. This is a sign of good architecture. And of course, with a module, we have access to different features such as filters, custom directives, and custom services.

Preparing data with filters

The filters are very handy when we want to prepare our data, prior to be displayed to the user. Let's say, for example, that we need to mention our title in uppercase once it reaches a length of more than 20 characters:

```
angular.module('HeaderModule', [])
.filter('customuppercase', function() {
  return function(input) {
    if(input.length > 20) {
      return input.toUpperCase();
    } else {
      return input;
    }
  };
})
.controller('HeaderController', function($scope) {
  $scope.title = "Hello world";
  $scope.updateTitle = function() {
    $scope.title = "That's a new title.";
  }
});
```

That's the definition of the custom filter called `customuppercase`. It receives the input and performs a simple check. What it returns, is what the user sees at the end. Here is how this filter could be used in HTML:

```
<h1>{{title | customuppercase}}</h1>
```

Of course, we may add more than one filter per variable. There are some predefined filters to limit the length, such as the JavaScript to JSON conversion or, for example, date formatting.

Dependency injection

Dependency management can be very tough sometimes. We may split everything into different modules/components. They have nicely written APIs and they are very well documented. However, very soon, we may realize that we need to create a lot of objects. Dependency injection solves this problem by providing what we need, on the fly. We already saw this in action. The `$scope` parameter passed to our controller, is actually created by the `injector` of AngularJS. To get something as a dependency, we need to define it somewhere and let the framework know about it. We do this as follows:

```
angular.module('HeaderModule', [])
.factory("Data", function() {
```

```
    return {
      getTitle: function() {
        return "A better title.";
      }
    }
  })
  .controller('HeaderController', function($scope, Data) {
    $scope.title = Data.getTitle();
    $scope.updateTitle = function() {
      $scope.title = "That's a new title.";
    }
  });
```

The `Module` class has a method called `factory`. It registers a new service that could later be used as a dependency. The function returns an object with only one method, `getTitle`. Of course, the name of the service should match the name of the controller's parameter. Otherwise, AngularJS will not be able to find the dependency's source.

The model in the context of AngularJS

In the well known Model-View-Controller pattern, the model is the part that stores the data in the application. AngularJS doesn't have a specific workflow to define models. The `$scope` variable could be considered a model. We keep the data in properties attached to the current scope. Later, we can use the `ng-model` directive and bind a property to the DOM element. We already saw how this works in the previous sections. The framework may not provide the usual form of a model, but it's made like that so that we can write our own implementation. The fact that AngularJS works with plain JavaScript objects, makes this task easily doable.

Final words on AngularJS

AngularJS is one of the leading frameworks, not only because it is made by Google, but also because it's really flexible. We could use just a small piece of it or build a solid architecture using the giant collection of features.

Selecting and initializing the database

To build a blog application, we need a database that will store the published articles. In most cases, the choice of the database depends on the current project. There are factors such as performance and scalability and we should keep them in mind. In order to have a better look at the possible solutions, we will have a look at the two of the most popular databases: **MongoDB** and **MySQL**. The first one is a NoSQL type of database. According to the Wikipedia entry (http://en.wikipedia.org/wiki/NoSQL) on NoSQL databases:

> *"A NoSQL or Not Only SQL database provides a mechanism for storage and retrieval of data that is modeled in means other than the tabular relations used in relational databases."*

In other words, it's simpler than a SQL database, and very often stores information in the key value type. Usually, such solutions are used when handling and storing large amounts of data. It is also a very popular approach when we need flexible schema or when we want to use JSON. It really depends on what kind of system we are building. In some cases, MySQL could be a better choice, while in some other cases, MongoDB. In our example blog, we're going to use both.

In order to do this, we will need a layer that connects to the database server and accepts queries. To make things a bit more interesting, we will create a module that has only one API, but can switch between the two database models.

Using NoSQL with MongoDB

Let's start with MongoDB. Before we start storing information, we need a MongoDB server running. It can be downloaded from the official page of the database https://www.mongodb.org/downloads.

We are not going to handle the communication with the database manually. There is a driver specifically developed for Node.js. It's called mongodb and we should include it in our package.json file. After successful installation via npm install, the driver will be available in our scripts. We can check this as follows:

```
"dependencies": {
  "mongodb": "1.3.20"
}
```

We will stick to the Model-View-Controller architecture and the database-related operations in a model called `Articles`. We can see this as follows:

```
var crypto = require("crypto"),
    type = "mongodb",
    client = require('mongodb').MongoClient,
    mongodb_host = "127.0.0.1",
    mongodb_port = "27017",
    collection;

module.exports = function() {
    if(type == "mongodb") {
        return {
            add: function(data, callback) { ... },
            update: function(data, callback) { ... },
            get: function(callback) { ... },
            remove: function(id, callback) { ... }
        }
    } else {
        return {
            add: function(data, callback) { ... },
            update: function(data, callback) { ... },
            get: function(callback) { ... },
            remove: function(id, callback) { ... }
        }
    }
}
```

It starts with defining a few dependencies and settings for the MongoDB connection. Line number one requires the `crypto` module. We will use it to generate unique IDs for every article. The `type` variable defines which database is currently accessed. The third line initializes the MongoDB driver. We will use it to communicate with the database server. After that, we set the host and port for the connection and at the end a global `collection` variable, which will keep a reference to the collection with the articles. In MongoDB, the collections are similar to the tables in MySQL. The next logical step is to establish a database connection and perform the needed operations, as follows:

```
connection = 'mongodb://';
connection += mongodb_host + ':' + mongodb_port;
connection += '/blog-application';
client.connect(connection, function(err, database) {
  if(err) {
    throw new Error("Can't connect");
```

```
    } else {
      console.log("Connection to MongoDB server successful.");
        collection = database.collection('articles');
    }
});
```

We pass the host and the port, and the driver is doing everything else. Of course, it is a good practice to handle the error (if any) and throw an exception. In our case, this is especially needed because without the information in the database, the frontend has nothing to show. The rest of the module contains methods to add, edit, retrieve, and delete records:

```
return {
  add: function(data, callback) {
    var date = new Date();
    data.id = crypto.randomBytes(20).toString('hex');
    data.date = date.getFullYear() + "-" + date.getMonth() + "-" +
date.getDate();
    collection.insert(data, {}, callback || function() {});
  },
  update: function(data, callback) {
    collection.update(
        {ID: data.id},
        data,
        {},
        callback || function(){ }
    );
  },
  get: function(callback) {
      collection.find({}).toArray(callback);
  },
  remove: function(id, callback) {
      collection.findAndModify(
          {ID: id},
          [],
          {},
          {remove: true},
          callback
      );
  }
}
```

The add and update methods accept the data parameter. That's a simple JavaScript object. For example, see the following code:

```
{
    title: "Blog post title",
    text: "Article's text here ..."
}
```

The records are identified by an automatically generated unique id. The update method needs it in order to find out which record to edit. All the methods also have a callback. That's important, because the module is meant to be used as a black box, that is, we should be able to create an instance of it, operate with the data, and at the end continue with the rest of the application's logic.

Using MySQL

We're going to use an SQL type of database with MySQL. We will add a few more lines of code to the already working Articles.js model. The idea is to have a class that supports the two databases like two different options. At the end, we should be able to switch from one to the other, by simply changing the value of a variable. Similar to MongoDB, we need to first install the database to be able use it. The official download page is http://www.mysql.com/downloads.

MySQL requires another Node.js module. It should be added again to the package. json file. We can see the module as follows:

```
"dependencies": {
    "mongodb": "1.3.20",
    "mysql": "2.0.0"
}
```

Similar to the MongoDB solution, we need to firstly connect to the server. To do so, we need to know the values of the **host**, **username**, and **password** fields. And because the data is organized in databases, a name of the database. In MySQL, we put our data into different databases. So, the following code defines the needed variables:

```
var mysql = require('mysql'),
    mysql_host = "127.0.0.1",
    mysql_user = "root",
    mysql_password = "",
    mysql_database = "blog_application",
    connection;
```

The previous example leaves the **password** field empty but we should set the proper value of our system. The MySQL database requires us to define a table and its fields before we start saving data. So, the following code is a short dump of the table used in this chapter:

```
CREATE TABLE IF NOT EXISTS `articles` (
  `id` int(11) NOT NULL AUTO_INCREMENT,
  `title` longtext NOT NULL,
  `text` longtext NOT NULL,
  `date` varchar(100) NOT NULL,
  PRIMARY KEY (`id`)
) ENGINE=InnoDB  DEFAULT CHARSET=utf8 AUTO_INCREMENT=1 ;
```

Once we have a database and its table set, we can continue with the database connection, as follows:

```
connection = mysql.createConnection({
    host: mysql_host,
    user: mysql_user,
    password: mysql_password
});
connection.connect(function(err) {
    if(err) {
        throw new Error("Can't connect to MySQL.");
    } else {
        connection.query("USE " + mysql_database, function(err, rows,
fields) {
            if(err) {
                throw new Error("Missing database.");
            } else {
                console.log("Successfully selected database.");
            }
        })
    }
});
```

The driver provides a method to connect to the server and execute queries. The first executed query selects the database. If everything is ok, you should see **Successfully selected database** as an output in your console. Half of the job is done. What we should do now is replicate the methods returned in the first MongoDB implementation. We need to do this because when we switch to the MySQL usage, the code using the class will not work. And by replicating them we mean that they should have the same names and should accept the same arguments.

If we do everything correctly, at the end our application will support two types of databases. And all we have to do is change the value of the type variable:

```
return {
    add: function(data, callback) {
        var date = new Date();
        var query = "";
        query += "INSERT INTO articles (title, text, date) VALUES (";
        query += connection.escape(data.title) + ", ";
        query += connection.escape(data.text) + ", ";
        query += "'" + date.getFullYear() + "-" + date.getMonth() +
    "-" + date.getDate() + "'";
        query += ")";
        connection.query(query, callback);
    },
    update: function(data, callback) {
        var query = "UPDATE articles SET ";
        query += "title=" + connection.escape(data.title) + ", ";
        query += "text=" + connection.escape(data.text) + " ";
        query += "WHERE id='" + data.id + "'";
        connection.query(query, callback);
    },
    get: function(callback) {
        var query = "SELECT * FROM articles ORDER BY id DESC";
        connection.query(query, function(err, rows, fields) {
            if(err) {
                throw new Error("Error getting.");
            } else {
                callback(rows);
            }
        });
    },
    remove: function(id, callback) {
        var query = "DELETE FROM articles WHERE id='" + id + "'";
        connection.query(query, callback);
    }
}
```

The code is a little longer than the one generated in the first MongoDB variant. That's because we needed to construct MySQL queries from the passed data. Keep in mind that we have to escape the information, which comes to the module. That's why we use `connection.escape()`. With these lines of code, our model is completed. Now we can add, edit, remove, or get data. Let's continue with the part that shows the articles to our users.

Developing the client side with AngularJS

Let's assume that there is some data in the database and we are ready to present it to the users. So far, we have only developed the model, which is the class that takes care of the access to the information. In the previous chapter of this book, we learned about Express. To simplify the process, we will use it again here. We need to first update the `package.json` file and include that in the framework, as follows:

```
"dependencies": {
  "express": "3.4.6",
  "jade": "0.35.0",
  "mongodb": "1.3.20",
  "mysql": "2.0.0"
}
```

We are also adding **Jade**, because we are going to use it as a template language. The writing of markup in plain HTML is not very efficient nowadays. By using the template engine, we can split the data and the HTML markup, which makes our application much better structured. Jade's syntax is kind of similar to HTML. We can write tags without the need to close them:

```
body
  p(class="paragraph", data-id="12").
    Sample text here
  footer
    a(href="#").
      my site
```

The preceding code snippet is transformed to the following code snippet:

```
<body>
  <p data-id="12" class="paragraph">Sample text here</p>
  <footer><a href="#">my site</a></footer>
</body>
```

Jade relies on the indentation in the content to distinguish the tags.

Let's start with the project structure, as seen in the following screenshot:

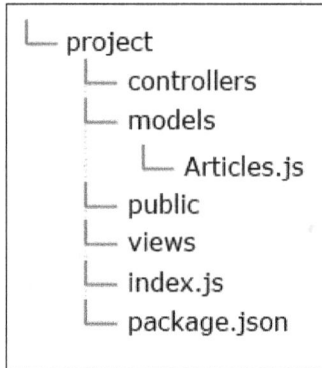

```
└── project
    └── controllers
    └── models
        └── Articles.js
    └── public
    └── views
    └── index.js
    └── package.json
```

We placed our already written class, Articles.js, inside the models directory. The public directory will contain CSS styles, and all the necessary client-side JavaScript: the AngularJS library, the AngularJS router module, and our custom code.

We will skip some of the explanations about the following code, because we already covered that in the previous chapter. Our index.js file looks as follows:

```
var express = require('express');
var app = express();
var articles = require("./models/Articles")();

app.set('views', __dirname + '/views');
app.set('view engine', 'jade');
app.use(express.static(__dirname + '/public'));

app.use(function(req, res, next) {
    req.articles = articles;
    next();
});

app.get('/api/get', require("./controllers/api/get"));
app.get('/', require("./controllers/index"));

app.listen(3000);
console.log('Listening on port 3000');
```

At the beginning, we require the Express framework and our model. Maybe it's better to initialize the model inside the controller, but in our case this is not necessary. Just after that, we set up some basic options for Express and define our own middleware. It has only one job to do and that is to attach the model to the request object. We are doing this because the request object is passed to all the route handlers. In our case, these handlers are actually the controllers. So, `Articles.js` becomes accessible everywhere via the `req.articles` property. At the end of the script, we placed two routes. The second one catches the usual requests that come from the users. The first one, `/api/get`, is a bit more interesting. We want to build our frontend on top of AngularJS. So, the data that is stored in the database should not enter the Node.js part but on the client side where we use Google's framework. To make this possible, we will create routes/controllers to get, add, edit, and delete records. Everything will be controlled by HTTP requests performed by AngularJS. In other words, we need an API.

Before we start using AngularJS, let's take a look at the `/controllers/api/get.js` controller:

```
module.exports = function(req, res, next) {
  req.articles.get(function(rows) {
    res.send(rows);
  });
}
```

The main job is done by our model and the response is handled by Express. It's nice because if we pass a JavaScript object, as we did, (`rows` is actually an array of objects) the framework sets the response headers automatically. To test the result, we could run the application with `node index.js` and open `http://localhost:3000/api/get`. If we don't have any records in the database, we will get an empty array. If not, the stored articles will be returned. So, that's the URL, which we should hit from within the AngularJS controller in order to get the information.

The code of the `/controller/index.js` controller is also just a few lines. We can see the code as follows:

```
module.exports = function(req, res, next) {
  res.render("list", { app: "" });
}
```

It simply renders the list view, which is stored in the `list.jade` file. That file should be saved in the `/views directory`. But before we see its code, we will check another file, which acts as a base for all the pages. Jade has a nice feature called *blocks*. We may define different partials and combine them into one template. The following is our `layout.jade file`:

```
doctype html
html(ng-app="#{app}")
  head
    title Blog
    link(rel='stylesheet', href='/style.css')
    script(src='/angular.min.js')
    script(src='/angular-route.min.js')
  body
    block content
```

There is only one variable passed to this template, which is #{app}. We will need it later to initialize the administration's module. The `angular.min.js` and `angular-route.min.js` files should be downloaded from the official AngularJS site, and placed in the `/public` directory. The body of the page contains a block placeholder called `content`, which we will later fill with the list of the articles. The following is the `list.jade` file:

```
extends layout
block content
  .container(ng-controller="BlogCtrl")
    section.articles
      article(ng-repeat="article in articles")
        h2
          {{article.title}}
          br
          small published on {{article.date}}
        p {{article.text}}
  script(src='/blog.js')
```

The two lines in the beginning combine both the templates into one page. The Express framework transforms the Jade template into HTML and serves it to the browser of the user. From there, the client-side JavaScript takes control. We are using the `ng-controller` directive saying that the `div` element will be controlled by an AngularJS controller called `BlogCtrl`. The same class should have variable, `articles`, filled with the information from the database. `ng-repeat` goes through the array and displays the content to the users. The `blog.js` class holds the code of the controller:

```
function BlogCtrl($scope, $http) {
  $scope.articles = [
```

```
      { title: "", text: "Loading ..."}
    ];
    $http({method: 'GET', url: '/api/get'})
    .success(function(data, status, headers, config) {
      $scope.articles = data;
      })
      .error(function(data, status, headers, config) {
        console.error("Error getting articles.");
    });
  }
```

The controller has two dependencies. The first one, $scope, points to the current view. Whatever we assign as a property there is available as a variable in our HTML markup. Initially, we add only one element, which doesn't have a title, but has text. It is shown to indicate that we are still loading the articles from the database. The second dependency, $http, provides an API in order to make HTTP requests. So, all we have to do is query /api/get, fetch the data, and pass it to the $scope dependency. The rest is done by AngularJS and its magical two-way data binding. To make the application a little more interesting, we will add a search field, as follows:

```
// views/list.jade
header
  .search
    input(type="text", placeholder="type a filter here", ng-
model="filterText")
  h1 Blog
  hr
```

The ng-model directive, binds the value of the input field to a variable inside our $scope dependency. However, this time, we don't have to edit our controller and can simply apply the same variable as a filter to the ng-repeat:

```
article(ng-repeat="article in articles | filter:filterText")
```

As a result, the articles shown will be filtered based on the user's input. Two simple additions, but something really valuable is on the page. The filters of AngularJS can be very powerful.

Implementing a control panel

The control panel is the place where we will manage the articles of the blog. Several things should be made in the backend before continuing with the user interface. They are as follows:

```
app.set("username", "admin");
app.set("password", "pass");
app.use(express.cookieParser('blog-application'));
app.use(express.session());
```

The previous lines of code should be added to `/index.js`. Our administration should be protected, so the first two lines define our credentials. We are using Express as data storage, simply creating key-value pairs. Later, if we need the username we can get it with `app.get("username")`. The next two lines enable session support. We need that because of the login process.

We added a middleware, which attaches the articles to the `request` object. We will do the same with the current user's status, as follows:

```
app.use(function(req, res, next) {
    if((
        req.session &&
        req.session.admin === true
    ) || (
        req.body &&
        req.body.username === app.get("username") &&
        req.body.password === app.get("password")
    )) {
        req.logged = true;
        req.session.admin = true;
    };
    next();
});
```

Our `if` statement is a little long, but it tells us whether the user is logged in or not. The first part checks whether there is a session created and the second one checks whether the user submitted a form with the correct username and password. If these expressions are `true`, then we attach a variable, `logged`, to the `request` object and create a session that will be valid during the following requests.

There is only one thing that we need in the main application's file. A few routes that will handle the control panel operations. In the following code, we are defining them along with the needed route handler:

```
var protect = function(req, res, next) {
    if(req.logged) {
        next();
    } else {
        res.send(401, 'No Access.');
    }
}
app.post('/api/add', protect, require("./controllers/api/add"));
app.post('/api/edit', protect, require("./controllers/api/edit"));
app.post('/api/delete', protect , require("./controllers/api/
delete"));
app.all('/admin', require("./controllers/admin"));
```

The three routes, which start with /api, will use the model `Articles.js` to add, edit, and remove articles from the database. These operations should be protected. We will add a middleware function that takes care of this. If the `req.logged` variable is not available, it simply responds with a `401 - Unauthorized` status code. The last route, /admin, is a little different because it shows a login form instead. The following is the controller to create new articles:

```
module.exports = function(req, res, next) {
    req.articles.add(req.body, function() {
        res.send({success: true});
    });
}
```

We transfer most of the logic to the frontend, so again, there are just a few lines. What is interesting here is that we pass `req.body` directly to the model. It actually contains the data submitted by the user. The following code, is how the `req.articles.add` method looks for the MongoDB implementation:

```
add: function(data, callback) {
    data.ID = crypto.randomBytes(20).toString('hex');
    collection.insert(data, {}, callback || function() {});
}
```

And the MySQL implementation is as follows:

```
add: function(data, callback) {
    var date = new Date();
    var query = "";
```

```
        query += "INSERT INTO articles (title, text, date) VALUES (";
        query += connection.escape(data.title) + ", ";
        query += connection.escape(data.text) + ", ";
        query += "'" + date.getFullYear() + "-" + date.getMonth() + "-" +
date.getDate() + "'";
        query += ")";
        connection.query(query, callback);
    }
```

In both the cases, we need `title` and `text` in the passed data object. Thankfully, due to Express' `bodyParser` middleware, this is what we have in the `req.body` object. We can directly forward it to the model. The other route handlers are almost the same:

```
// api/edit.js
module.exports = function(req, res, next) {
    req.articles.update(req.body, function() {
        res.send({success: true});
    });
}
```

What we changed is the method of the `Articles.js` class. It is not `add` but `update`. The same technique is applied in the route to delete an article. We can see it as follows:

```
// api/delete.js
module.exports = function(req, res, next) {
    req.articles.remove(req.body.id, function() {
        res.send({success: true});
    });
}
```

What we need for deletion is not the whole body of the request but only the unique ID of the record. Every API method sends `{success: true}` as a response. While we are dealing with API requests, we should always return a response. Even if something goes wrong.

The last thing in the Node.js part, which we have to cover, is the controller responsible for the user interface of the administration panel, that is, the. /controllers/admin.js file:

```
module.exports = function(req, res, next) {
    if(req.logged) {
        res.render("admin", { app: "admin" });
    } else {
        res.render("login", { app: "" });
    }
}
```

There are two templates that are rendered: `/views/admin.jade` and `/views/login.jade`. Based on the variable, which we set in `/index.js`, the script decides which one to show. If the user is not logged in, then a login form is sent to the browser, as follows:

```
extends layout
block content
  .container
    header
      h1 Administration
     hr
    section.articles
      article
        form(method="post", action="/admin")
        span Username:
        br
        input(type="text", name="username")
        br
        span Password:
        br
        input(type="password", name="password")
        br
        br
        input(type="submit", value="login")
```

There is no AngularJS code here. All we have is the good old HTML form, which submits its data via POST to the same URL—`/admin`. If the username and password are correct, the `.logged` variable is set to `true` and the controller renders the other template:

```
extends layout
block content
  .container
    header
      h1 Administration
      hr
      a(href="/") Public
      span  |
      a(href="#/") List
      span  |
      a(href="#/add") Add
    section(ng-view)
  script(src='/admin.js')
```

The control panel needs several views to handle all the operations. AngularJS has a great router module, which works with hashtags-type URLs, that is, URLs such as / admin#/add. The same module requires a placeholder for the different partials. In our case, this is a section tag. The ng-view attribute tells the framework that this is the element prepared for that logic. At the end of the template, we are adding an external file, which keeps the whole client-side JavaScript code that is needed by the control panel.

While the client-side part of the applications needs only loading of the articles, the control panel requires a lot more functionalities. It is good to use the modular system of AngularJS. We need the routes and views to change, so the ngRoute module is needed as a dependency. This module is not added in the main angular.min.js build. It is placed in the angular-route.min.js file. The following code shows how our module starts:

```
var admin = angular.module('admin', ['ngRoute']);
admin.config(['$routeProvider',
  function($routeProvider) {
    $routeProvider
    .when('/', {})
    .when('/add', {})
    .when('/edit/:id', {})
    .when('/delete/:id', {})
    .otherwise({
        redirectTo: '/'
      });
  }
]);
```

We configured the router by mapping URLs to specific routes. At the moment, the routes are just empty objects, but we will fix that shortly. Every controller will need to make HTTP requests to the Node.js part of the application. It will be nice if we have such a service and use it all over our code. We can see an example as follows:

```
admin.factory('API', function($http) {
  var request = function(method, url) {
    return function(callback, data) {
      $http({method: method, url: url, data: data})
      .success(callback)
        .error(function(data, status, headers, config) {
          console.error("Error requesting '" + url + "'.");
      });
    }
  }
```

```
    return {
      get: request('GET', '/api/get'),
      add: request('POST', '/api/add'),
      edit: request('POST', '/api/edit'),
      remove: request('POST', '/api/delete')
    }
  });
```

One of the best things about AngularJS is that it works with plain JavaScript objects. There are no unnecessary abstractions and no extending or inheriting special classes. We are using the `.factory` method to create a simple JavaScript object. It has four methods that can be called: `get`, `add`, `edit`, and `remove`. Each one of them calls a function, which is defined in the helper method `request`. The service has only one dependency, `$http`. We already know this module; it handles HTTP requests nicely. The URLs that we are going to query are the same ones that we defined in the Node.js part.

Now, let's create a controller that will show the articles currently stored in the database. First, we should replace the empty route object `.when('/', {})` with the following object:

```
.when('/', {
  controller: 'ListCtrl',
  template: '\
    <article ng-repeat="article in articles">\
      <hr />\
      <strong>{{article.title}}</strong><br />\
        (<a href="#/edit/{{article.id}}">edit</a>)\
        (<a href="#/delete/{{article.id}}">remove</a>)\
      </article>\
    '
})
```

The object has to contain a controller and a template. The template is nothing more than a few lines of HTML markup. It looks a bit like the template used to show the articles on the client side. The difference is the links used to edit and delete. JavaScript doesn't allow new lines in the string definitions. The backward slashes at the end of the lines prevent syntax errors, which will eventually be thrown by the browser. The following is the code for the controller. It is defined, again, in the module:

```
admin.controller('ListCtrl', function($scope, API) {
  API.get(function(articles) {
    $scope.articles = articles;
  });
});
```

And here is the beauty of the AngularJS dependency injection. Our custom-defined service API is automatically initialized and passed to the controller. The .get method fetches the articles from the database. Later, we send the information to the current $scope dependency and the two-way data binding does the rest. The articles are shown on the page.

The work with AngularJS is so easy that we could combine the controller to add and edit in one place. Let's store the route object in an external variable, as follows:

```
var AddEditRoute = {
  controller: 'AddEditCtrl',
    template: '\
      <hr />\
      <article>\
        <form>\
        <span>Title</spna><br />\
        <input type="text" ng-model="article.title"/><br />\
        <span>Text</spna><br />\
        <textarea rows="7" ng-model="article.text"></textarea>\
        <br /><br />\
        <button ng-click="save()">save</button>\
        </form>\
      </article>\
    '
};
```

And later, assign it to the both the routes, as follows:

```
.when('/add', AddEditRoute)
.when('/edit/:id', AddEditRoute)
```

The template is just a form with the necessary fields and a button, which calls the save method in the controller. Notice that we bound the input field and the text area to variables inside the $scope dependency. This comes in handy because we don't need to access the DOM to get the values. We can see this as follows:

```
admin.controller(
  'AddEditCtrl',
  function($scope, API, $location, $routeParams) {
    var editMode = $routeParams.id ? true : false;
    if(editMode) {
      API.get(function(articles) {
        articles.forEach(function(article) {
          if(article.id == $routeParams.id) {
            $scope.article = article;
```

```
            }
        });
    });
}
$scope.save = function() {
    API[editMode ? 'edit' : 'add'](function() {
        $location.path('/');
    }, $scope.article);
}
})
```

The controller receives four dependencies. We already know about $scope and API. The $location dependency is used when we want to change the current route, or, in other words, to forward the user to another view. The $routeParams dependency is needed to fetch parameters from the URL. In our case, /edit/:id is a route with a variable inside. Inside the code, the id is available in $routeParams.id. The adding and editing of articles uses the same form. So, with a simple check, we know what the user is currently doing. If the user is in the edit mode, then we fetch the article based on the provided id and fill the form. Otherwise, the fields are empty and new records will be created.

The deletion of an article can be done by using a similar approach, which is adding a route object and defining a new controller. We can see the deletion as follows:

```
.when('/delete/:id', {
    controller: 'RemoveCtrl',
    template: ' '
})
```

We don't need a template in this case. Once the article is deleted from the database, we will forward the user to the list page. We have to call the remove method of the API. Here is how the RemoveCtrl controller looks like:

```
admin.controller(
    'RemoveCtrl',
    function($scope, $location, $routeParams, API) {
        API.remove(function() {
            $location.path('/');
        }, $routeParams);
    }
);
```

The preceding code depicts same dependencies like in the previous controller. This time, we simply forward the $routeParams dependency to the API. And because it is a plain JavaScript object, everything works as expected.

Summary

In this chapter, we built a simple blog by writing the backend of the application in Node.js. The module for database communication, which we wrote, can work with the MongoDB or MySQL database and store articles. The client-side part and the control panel of the blog were developed with AngularJS. We then defined a custom service using the built-in HTTP and routing mechanisms.

Node.js works well with AngularJS, mainly because both are written in JavaScript. We found out that AngularJS is built to support the developer. It removes all those boring tasks such as DOM element referencing, attaching event listeners, and so on. It's a great choice for the modern client-side coding stack.

In the next chapter, we will see how to program a real-time chat with Socket.IO, one of the popular solutions covering the WebSockets communication.

4
Developing a Chat with Socket.IO

As we learned in the previous chapter, Node.js collaborates really well with frontend frameworks such as AngularJS. It's great that we can transfer data from the browser to Node.js and vice-versa. It's even better if we can do in this real time. Nowadays, real-time communication is heavily integrated in almost every web product. It gives a nice user experience and brings a lot of benefits to the application's owners. Usually, when we talk about real-time web components, we mean **WebSockets**. WebSocket is a protocol that allows us to establish a two-way (bidirectional) conversation between the browser and the server. This opens a whole new world and gives us the power to implement fast and robust apps. **Node.js** supports WebSockets, and we will see how to build a real-time chat with WebSockets. The application will use Socket.IO. It is a library that is built on top of WebSockets and provides mechanisms to cover the same functionalities if they are not available. We will have an input field, and every user who opens the page will be able to send messages to every other user who is available.

In this chapter, we will learn how to set up Socket.IO and how to use it in a browser and start a Node.js server, making real-time chat possible.

Exploring WebSockets and Socket.IO

Let's say that we want to build a chat feature. The first thing that we should do is to develop the part that shows the messages on the screen. In a typical scenario, we want these messages to be delivered fast, that is, almost immediately after they were sent. However, if we don't use sockets to receive the data from the server, we need to make an HTTP request. Also, the server should keep the information till we request it to do so. So, imagine what would happen if we had 10 users and each one of them starts sending data.

We need to maintain a user session in order to identify the user's requests. These problems are easily solved if we use sockets. Once the socket is opened, we have a long live channel, and we can send messages back and forth. This means that you can start receiving information without requesting it. The architecture is analogous to a big net of bridges. The bridge is always open, and if we need to go somewhere, we are free to do so. At the center of the net, we have a hub that connects every side with each other. In the context of the web, the hub is our server. Every time we need to reach some of the users attached to the net, we just need to send a message via the socket. The server receives it and bypasses it to the right person. This is one of the most effective ways to implement real-time communication. It saves time and resources.

As it happens with most of the cool technologies, we don't need to start from scratch and write low-level stuff, such as handshake requests for example. There are two types of developers: those who work really hard and abstract the complex things into simpler APIs and tools, and those who know how to use them. Developers in the second group can make use of libraries such as Socket.IO. This chapter deals extensively with the Socket.IO module. It acts as an abstraction over WebSockets and simplifies the process to a great extent.

Before we continue, **Socket.IO** is actually more than a layer over **WebSockets**. In practice, it does a lot more, as mentioned on the website at `http://socket.io/`:

> *"Socket.IO aims to make realtime apps possible in every browser and mobile device, blurring the differences between the different transport mechanisms. It's care-free realtime 100% in JavaScript."*

There are some common situations that we usually encounter with the protocol, for example, heartbeats, timeouts, and disconnection support. All these events are not natively supported by the WebSocket API. Thankfully, Socket.IO is here to solve these issues. The library also eliminates some cross-browser problems and makes sure that your app works everywhere.

Understanding the basic application structure

In the previous chapter, we used Express and Jade to write the delivery of the assets (HTML, CSS, and JavaScript) of the application. Here, we will stick to pure JavaScript code and will avoid the usage of additional dependencies. The only thing that we need to add to our `package.json` file is Socket.IO:

```
{
  "name": "projectname",
```

```
    "description": "description",
    "version": "0.0.1",
    "dependencies": {
        "socket.io": "latest"
    }
}
```

After we call `npm install` in our project's folder, Socket.IO is placed in a newly created `node_modules` directory. Let's create two new directories. The following screenshot shows what the application file structure should look like:

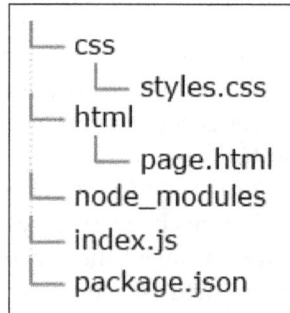

```
└── css
        └── styles.css
└── html
        └── page.html
└── node_modules
└── index.js
└── package.json
```

The file structure

The application will read the `styles.css` file and deliver its content to the browser. The same thing will happen with `/html/page.html`, which is the file that contains the HTML markup of the project. The Node.js code goes to `/index.js`.

Running the server

Before we start using Socket.IO, let's first write a simple Node.js server code, which responds with the chat's page. We can see the server code as follows:

```
var http = require('http'),
    fs = require('fs'),
    port = 3000,
    html = fs.readFileSync(__dirname + '/html/page.html', {encoding:
'utf8'}),
    css = fs.readFileSync(__dirname + '/css/styles.css', {encoding:
'utf8'});

var app = http.createServer(function (req, res) {
    if(req.url === '/styles.css') {
        res.writeHead(200, {'Content-Type': 'text/css'});
        res.end(css);
```

```
  } else {
    res.writeHead(200, {'Content-Type': 'text/html'});
    res.end(html);
  }
}).listen(port, '127.0.0.1');
```

The preceding code should be placed in /index.js. The script starts with the definition of several global variables. The http module is used to create the server, and the fs module is used to read the CSS and HTML files from the disk. The html and css variables contain the actual code that will be sent to the browser. In our case, this data is static. That's why we are reading the files only once, that is, when the script is run. We are also doing this synchronously by using fs.readFileSync and not fs.readFile. Just after this, our server is initialized and run. The req.url variable contains the currently requested file. According to its value, we respond to it with proper content. Once the server is run, the HTML and CSS code stays the same. If we change something, we need to stop and start the script again. That's because we are reading the file's content before we start the server. This could be considered as a good practice if there are no changes in /css/styles.css or /html/page.html. Inserting the fs.readFileSync operations in the server's handler will make our chat a bit slow because we will read from the disk during every request.

Adding Socket.IO

The implementation of the chat requires the code to be written in both places: at the server side and the client side. We will continue with the Node.js part by extending the previous code, as follows:

```
var io = require('socket.io').listen(app);
io.sockets.on('connection', function (socket) {
  socket.emit('welcome', { message: 'Welcome!' });
  socket.on('send', function (data) {
      io.sockets.emit('receive', data);
  });
});
```

The http.createServer method returns a new web server object. We have to pass this object to Socket.IO. Once everything is done, we have access to the wonderful and simple API. We may listen for incoming events and send messages to the users who are attached to the server. The io.sockets property refers to all the sockets created in the system, while the socket object, passed as an argument to the connection handler, represents only one individual user.

For example, in the preceding code, we are listening for the `connection` event, that is, for a new user to connect to the server. When this happens, the server sends a personal message to that user that reads `Welcome!`

The next thing that may happen is we receive a new type of message from the user, our script should distribute this information to all the available sockets. That's what `io.sockets.emit` does. Keep in mind that the `emit` method may receive our own custom event names and data. It is not necessary to strictly follow the format used here.

Writing the client side of the chat

Having completed writing the code for the server side, we can now continue writing for the frontend, that is, write the necessary HTML and JavaScript that will communicate with the chat server.

Preparing the HTML markup

With the development done so far, our chat feature would look like the following screenshot:

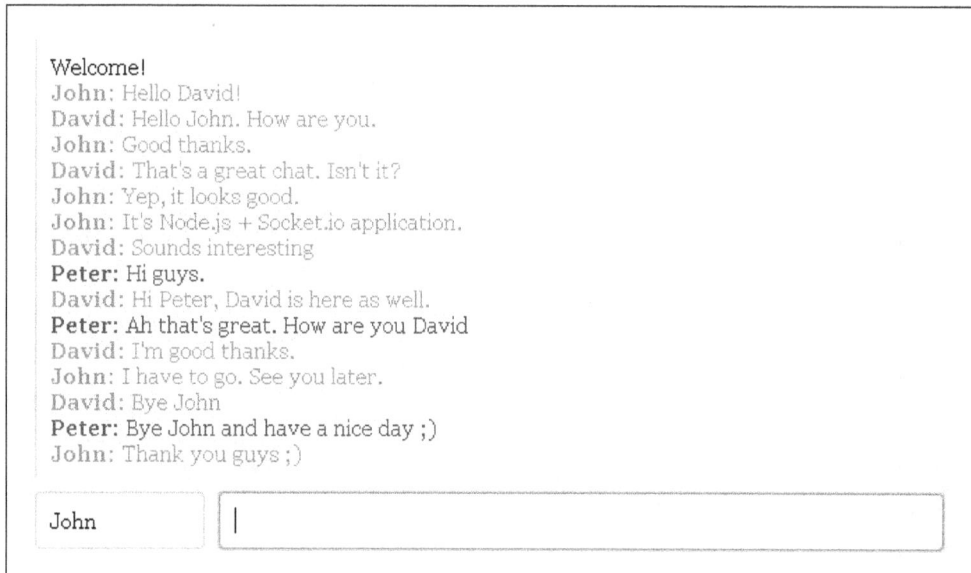

Welcome!
John: Hello David!
David: Hello John. How are you.
John: Good thanks.
David: That's a great chat. Isn't it?
John: Yep, it looks good.
John: It's Node.js + Socket.io application.
David: Sounds interesting
Peter: Hi guys.
David: Hi Peter, David is here as well.
Peter: Ah that's great. How are you David
David: I'm good thanks.
John: I have to go. See you later.
David: Bye John
Peter: Bye John and have a nice day ;)
John: Thank you guys ;)

John

We have a container that acts as a holder for the incoming messages. There are two input boxes. The first one is for the name of the user and the second one accepts the message that we have to send. Every user has a random color applied to his/her texts. There is no button to send the data to the server; we can do this by pressing the *Enter* key. Let's continue to read the HTML markup saved in /html/page.html shown as follows:

```html
<!doctype html>
<html>
    <head>
        <link rel="stylesheet" type="text/css" href="styles.css">
    </head>
    <body>
        <section>
          <div id="chat"></div>
          <input type="text" id="name" placeholder="your name" />
          <input type="text" id="input" disabled="disabled" />
        </section>
        <script src="/socket.io/socket.io.js"></script>
    <script>
      window.onload = function() {
        var Chat = (function() {
          // ...
        })();
      }
    </script>
    </body>
</html>
```

The CSS styles are added at the top of the page and to the scripts at the bottom. There are just three elements that represent the controls mentioned in the previous code. The bootstrap of the logic is placed in a window.onload handler. We are doing this just to be sure that all the assets are fully loaded. Note that the input field, which will accept the message, is disabled by default. Once the socket connection is established, we will enable it. There is one last thing that we should clarify — the location/source where the /socket.io/socket.io.js file is coming from. It is not downloaded and saved in the project directories from an external source; it is delivered at that location by Socket.IO. That's one of the reasons behind passing the web server object to Socket.IO at the backend.

Writing the chat logic

The HTML markup itself is useless. The next step in our development process will be writing the JavaScript code that will communicate with the backend. We will need to catch the user's input and send it to the server. The messages displayed on the screen will be painted in different colors. We will start by defining two helper methods as follows:

```
var addEventListener = function(obj, evt, fnc) {
    if (obj.addEventListener) { // W3C model
        obj.addEventListener(evt, fnc, false);
        return true;
    } else if (obj.attachEvent) { // Microsoft model
        return obj.attachEvent('on' + evt, fnc);
    }
}
var getRandomColor = function() {
    var letters = '0123456789ABCDEF'.split('');
    var color = '#';
    for (var i = 0; i < 6; i++ ) {
        color += letters[Math.round(Math.random() * 15)];
    }
    return color;
}
```

The first one, `addEventListener` function, will add an event listener to a DOM element. To make our chat work in Internet Explorer, we need to use `attachEvent` instead of `addEventListener`. The second, `getRandomColor` function, delivers a different color every time. We will use this to distinguish messages from the different users.

Our client-side logic starts with the defining of a few variables:

```
var socket = io.connect('http://localhost:3000'),
    chat = document.querySelector("#chat"),
    input = document.querySelector("#input"),
    name = document.querySelector("#name"),
    color = getRandomColor();
```

We will use the `socket` variable to communicate with the server. The next three variables are shortcuts to the previously used DOM elements. It is recommended to create such shortcuts because referencing elements all the time with `document.getElementById` or `document.querySelector` may cause of performance issues.

The chat does two things: it sends messages to the Node.js part and receives messages from there. Let's wrap everything into two simple functions, as follows:

```
var send = function(message) {
  var username = name.value === '' ? '' : '<strong>' +
    name.value + ': </strong>';
  socket.emit('send', {
    message: '<span style="color:' + color + '">' +
                    username + message + '</span>'
  });
}

var display = function(message) {
  chat.innerHTML = chat.innerHTML + message + '<br />';
  chat.scrollTop = chat.scrollHeight;
}
```

Here, we are sending the message via the `socket.emit` method and wrapping the text in a colored `span` element. Of course, if the user types in something in the `name` input field, we use the value and send it along with the rest of the data. The `display` function is pretty simple. It just changes the `innerHTML` property of the `chat` element. What is interesting is the second line. If we use the chat feature a bit, we will notice that `div` will be filled out very soon, and what we actually see are only the first messages. By setting the `scrollTop` property to `scrollHeight`, we make sure that the holder will be always scrolled downwards.

The next step in our small application is handling the user's input. This can be done using the following code:

```
addEventListener(input, "keydown", function(e) {
  if(e.keyCode === 13) {
    send(input.value);
    input.value = "";
  }
});
```

The only one key that is interesting for us at the moment is the *Enter* key. Its key code is 13. If the key is pressed, the value of the field is emitted to the server. We are flushing the input field to allow the user to type in a new message.

The last thing that we should do is write the code to receive the messages:

```
socket.on('welcome', function (data) {
  display(data.message);
  input.removeAttribute("disabled");
```

```
  input.focus();
}).on('receive', function(data) {
  display(data.message);
});
```

There are two types of events that we are listening to. They are `welcome` and `receive`. The `welcome` event is sent when the connection is established. The `receive` event is an incoming event, when some of the users send a message (including ourselves). We may ask why we need to send our own message to the server and receive it after that. Isn't it easier to place the text directly onto the holder? The answer to this is that we need consistency of the data, that is, we should provide the same message in absolutely the same order to all the users. This can be guaranteed by only one piece of the app and that's the server.

With this last code snippet, we have finished building our chat feature. In the last part of this chapter, we will improve user-to-user communication.

Implementing user-to-user communication

Our chat is now functioning, but it would be nice if we could send a message to one specific user. Such a feature requires changes in both places: at the frontend and backend. Let's first change the Node.js script.

Changing the server-side code

So far, the users were anonymous in our system. We just passed the received message to all the sockets available. However, to implement a user-to-user conversation, we need to set unique ID for every user. Along with that, we have to keep references to all the created sockets so that we can emit messages to them. This can be done as follows:

```
var crypto = require('crypto');
var users = [];
```

We can make use of the `crypto` module, which is available by default in Node.js to generate the random unique IDs, as follows:

```
var id = crypto.randomBytes(20).toString('hex');
```

We should also notify the people in the chat about the available users. Otherwise, they will not be able to pick an appropriate user to chat with. The notification is done as follows:

```
var sendUsers = function() {
  io.sockets.emit('users', users.map(function(user) {
    return { id: user.id, name: user.username };
  }));
}
```

The user's name was actually passed along with the message. It was a part of the message, and the backend doesn't use it at all. However, in the new scenario, we need it with the ID. The previous code sends the users array to the browser, but before that, it filters it and passes only the ID and the name. As we will see in the following code, we also have a `socket` property for every element. The following is the updated `connection` handler:

```
io.sockets.on('connection', function (socket) {
  var id = crypto.randomBytes(20).toString('hex');
  users.push({ socket: socket, id: id, name: null });
  socket.emit('welcome', { message: 'Welcome!', id: id });
  sendUsers();
  socket.on('send', function (data) {
    if(data.username !== '') {
      setUsername(id, data.username);
    }
    if(data.toUser !== '') {
      users.forEach(function(user) {
      if(user.id === data.toUser || user.id === data.fromUser) {
        user.socket.emit('receive', data);
      }
    })
    } else {
      io.sockets.emit('receive', data);
    }
  });
});
```

So, a new user connection is received at the server. We generate a new ID and create a new element inside the `users` array. We keep the socket, the ID, and the name of the user. After that, we emit the good old `welcome` message, but this time we send the ID as well. Now, the frontend can identify itself into the system, and because the `users` variable is updated, we should notify the rest of the world about this via the `sendUsers` function. We start listening for the `send` message, and once it comes, we update the user's name in the array with the `setUsername` method, as follows:

```
var setUsername = function(id, name) {
    users.forEach(function(user) {
        if(user.id === id) {
            user.username = name;
            sendUsers();
        }
    });
}
```

The subsequent lines check whether there is a `toUser` property. If there is one, we know that it contains IDs of some of the other users. So, we simply find the user ID and pass the message to the exact socket. If there is no `toUser` property, then the data is again sent to everyone using `io.sockets.emit('receive', data)`. Together with `toUser`, the frontend should also send `fromUser`. That's because normally the guy who sends the text doesn't see its message on the screen until the server sends it back. We will use `fromUser` to achieve this.

Making changes to the frontend of the chat

The first thing we have to do is to show the available users on the screen so that we can choose one of them to chat with. Just below the input fields, we will add a drop-down menu, as follows:

```
<select id="users">
    <option value="">all</option>
</select>
```

We will need a few new variables defined. A new shortcut to the `select` element, the currently selected user from the list, and a variable that will hold the current user's ID. This is done as follows:

```
var users = document.querySelector("#users"),
    selectedUser = null,
    id = null;
```

The `send` method has changed a bit. We can see it as follows:

```
var send = function(message) {
  var username = name.value == '' ? '' : '<strong>' +
    name.value + ': </strong>';
  socket.emit('send', {
    message: '<span style="color:' + color + '">' + username +
      message + '</span>',
    username: name.value,
    toUser: users.value,
    fromUser: id
    });
}
```

The difference is that we are sending the user's name in a separate property, that is, the ID of the user and the ID of the user we want to chat with. If there is no such user, then the value is just an empty string. The `display` method can stay the same. We need one more event listener for the drop-down menu changes. We will add it as follows:

```
addEventListener(users, "change", function(e) {
  selectedUser = users.value;
});
```

Most of the work is done in the listeners of the socket object:

```
socket.on('welcome', function (data) {
  id = data.id;
  display(data.message);
  input.removeAttribute("disabled");
  input.focus();
}).on('receive', function(data) {
  display(data.message);
}).on('users', function(data) {
  var html = '<option value="">all</option>';
  for(var i=0; i<data.length; i++) {
    var user = data[i];
    if(id != user.id) {
      var username = user.name ? user.name : 'user' + (i+1);
      var selected = user.id === selectedUser ? '
selected="selected"': '';
      html += '<option value="' + user.id + '"' + selected + '>' +
username + '</option>';
```

```
      }
   }
   users.innerHTML = html;
});
```

First, the `welcome` message is received. It comes with the ID, so we will store it in our local variable. We show the welcome message, enable the input, and bring the focus there. No changes here. What is new is the last message listener. That's the place where we populate the drop-down menu with data. We compose an HTML string and set it as a value of the `innerHTML` property at the end. There are two checks. The first one prevents the current user from showing in the `select` element. The second condition automatically selects a user from the list. This is actually quite important because the user's message can be sent many times and the menu should maintain its selection.

Summary

In this chapter, we've learned how to create a real-time chat by using Socket.IO. It's a great Node.js module that simplifies work with WebSockets. It is a technology that is widely used today and is part of the future's applications.

In the next chapter, we will learn how to use Backbone.js to create a simple to-do application. Again, we will manage the data with the help of Node.js.

5
Creating a To-do Application with Backbone.js

In the previous chapters, we learned how to create real-time chat with Socket.IO. We made a blog application with AngularJS and used Express to create a simple website. This chapter is dedicated to another popular framework—Backbone.js. Backbone.js is one of the first JavaScript frameworks that gained popularity. There are models that deal with the data, views that control the logic and the user interface, and the built-in router that handles the changes in the browser's address. The framework plays really well with jQuery, which makes it attractive to almost every JavaScript developer. In this chapter, we are going to build a simple application for storing short tasks. At the end, we will be able to create, edit, delete tasks, and mark them as finished.

In this chapter, we will cover the following topics:

- The basics of Backbone.js
- Writing the Node.js code that manages the to-do lists
- Coding the frontend using Backbone.js

Exploring the Backbone.js framework

Before starting with the example's application, we should check out the main features of the framework. Sometimes, it's good to know what is going on under the hood. So, let's dive in.

Recognizing the framework dependency

Most of the software that we use nowadays is built on top of other libraries or tools. Normally, they are called **dependencies**. Backbone.js has only one hard dependency — that's Underscore.js, which is a library full of utility functions. There are functions such as `forEach`, `map`, or `union` for arrays. We can extend an object and retrieve its keys or values. All these are functionalities we need sometimes, but they are missing in the built-in JavaScript objects. So, we should include the library in our page. Otherwise, Backbone.js will throw an error because of the missing functionalities.

Backbone.js works really well with jQuery. It checks whether the library is available and starts using it right away. It's a nice collaboration because we can speed up our work with the various jQuery methods. It's not a must-have dependency and the framework still works without it, but it simplifies the DOM manipulations.

Extending the functionality

The framework has a few independent components that we will use. So, the idea is that we will create new classes that inherit the functionality of the base implementations. These components have the `extend` method, which accepts an object — our custom logic. At the end, our properties will overwrite the original code. The following is a new view class that we will create:

```
var ListView = Backbone.View.extend({
  render: function() {
    // ...
  }
});
var list = new ListView();
```

There are no mandatory modules. There is no strictly defined central entry point of our application. Everything is up to us, which is good. All the parts are so decoupled, which makes Backbone.js easy to work with.

Understanding Backbone.js as an event-driven framework

By event driven, we mean that the application flow is determined by events, that is, every class/object in the framework dispatches messages that notify the rest of the components about some action. In other words, every object we create can accept listeners and can trigger events. This makes our application extremely flexible and communicative. This approach encourages modular programming, and it really helps in building solid architectures. The `Backbone.Events` module is a module that delivers this functionality. The following example code explains how we can extend the `Backbone.Events` module:

```
var object = {};
_.extend(object, Backbone.Events);
object.on("event", function(msg) {
  console.log(msg);
});
object.trigger("event", "an event");
```

Underscore.js `extend` method merges the passed objects into one. In our case, we will produce an object that has the observer pattern implemented. This leads us to conclude that every view, model, or collection produced by Backbone.js has the `on` and `trigger` methods available.

Using models

The model is an important part of every Backbone.js project. Its primary function is to hold our data. The model keeps, validates, and synchronizes data with the server. Together with this, the model can notify the outside world of the events that happen inside the module. The following example code explains how we can extend the `Backbone.Model` module:

```
var User = Backbone.Model.extend({
  defaults: {
    name: '',
    password: '',
    isAdmin: false
  }
});
var user = new User({
  name: 'John',
  password: '1234'
});
console.log(user.get('name'));
```

The information in the model is kept in a hash table. There are properties and values. We have the set and get methods to access the data. Once something is changed, the model triggers an event. You may wonder why we need to wrap the data into a class. In the beginning, Backbone.Model looks like an unnecessary abstraction. However, very soon you will realize that such a concept is really powerful. First, we can attach as many views as we want to the same model, and by attach we mean listening to a change event. We can update the model and change the user interface as well. The second thing is that we can connect the model to a server-side API and immediately synchronize the information via an Ajax request. We will do this in an example application later.

Using collections

Very often, we will need to store the models in an array. The collections are made for such cases. The Backbone.Collection module has methods such as add, remove, and forEach for interaction with the stored items. It can also fetch multiple models from an external source and that's what it is used mostly for. Of course, the collection needs to know what is the type of the model. The following example code explains how we can extend the Backbone.Collection module:

```
var User = Backbone.Model.extend({
  defaults: {
    name: '',
    password: '',
    isAdmin: false
  }
});
var Accounts = Backbone.Collection.extend({
  model: User
});
var accounts = new Accounts();
accounts.add({name: 'John'});
accounts.add({name: 'Steve'});
accounts.add({name: 'David'});
accounts.forEach(function(model) {
  console.log(model.get('name'));
});
```

The example shows the same User model class, but this is placed inside a collection. We can easily add new users and retrieve their names. Similar to the Backbone. Model module, every collection can sync our data with an external server via HTTP requests.

Implementing views

The views in Backbone.js take care of the user interface and its business logic, that is, when compared to the usual **Model-View-Controller** (**MVC**) pattern, here, the view and the controller are merged in one place. Again, there is a base class that we have to extend. An interesting thing is that a DOM element is automatically created for us. We can control its type, class, or ID, and it is always there. This is really handy because we can build our interface dynamically behind the scenes and add it to the page only once, avoiding the multiple reflows and repaints of the browser. This can increase the performance of our application.

There is a certain popular wrong implementation of Backbone.js views. I myself made a lot of mistakes till I understood how everything is supposed to work. The idea is to bind the view's `render` method to a change in the model. By doing this, the interface will be automatically updated. It is also important to find the balance and keep the classes short. Sometimes, we may end up with a really long view, which controls a big portion of our page. A good practice is to divide the parts into smaller pieces. It's just a lot easier for maintenance and testing. The following example code explains how we can extend the `Backbone.View` module:

```
var LabelView = Backbone.View.extend({
  tagName: 'span'
});
var label = new LabelView();
console.log(label.el);
```

The `tagName` property determines the type of the generated DOM element. It's a good practice to operate only with that created element. It's not a good idea to attach it to another view or somewhere in the DOM tree. This should happen outside the class. There are some tricky sections we must watch out for when we need to attach event listeners, for example, `click`. However, the framework has a solution for such cases. We will see it later in this chapter.

Using the router

So far, we learned about models, collections, and views. There is one more thing that is widely used, especially when we need to build a single-page application like ours—the router. It's a module that maps a function to a specific URL. It supports the new history API so that it can handle addresses such as `/page/action/32`. The HTML5 history API is a standardized way to manipulate the browser history via a script. If the browser doesn't support this API, then it works with the good old fragment version, that is, `#page/action/32`.

The following example code explains how we can extend the
`Backbone.Router` module:

```
var Workspace = Backbone.Router.extend({
  routes: {
    "help":                  "help",
    "search/:query":         "search",
    "search/:query/p:page":  "search"
  },
  help: function() {
    // ...
  },
  search: function(query, page) {
    // ...
  }
});
```

We just have to define our routes and the module is responsible for the rest. Keep
in mind that we may use dynamic URLs, that is, URLs that contain dynamic parts,
like with the `search` route in the preceding code.

The router itself collaborates with another module called `Backbone.history`. This
is the class that listens to `hashchange` events or `pushState` events triggered by the
browser. So, once the routes are initialized, we should run `Backbone.history.`
`start()` in order to fire the matched route handler. We will see this in action
while writing the client-side part of the application.

Talking to the backend

As we mentioned, Backbone.js offers automatic synchronization with the server-
side data. This, of course, needs some efforts from our side, and they are more like
the things we need to do at the backend part of the application. The client-side
JavaScript makes **CRUD** (**create**, **read**, **update**, and **delete**) HTTP requests and the
server will process them. Every model and collection should have a `url` property
(or method) set, and we will send the information to this address. It's only one
URL, so the different operations are using different request methods—GET, POST,
PUT, and DELETE. In our example, the key moment is to wire Backbone.js's objects
to the Node.js server. Once this is done, we will be able to manage the to-do lists
easily directly from the browser.

Writing the backend of the application

The backend is the Node.js part, which will take care of the data delivery and will serve the necessary HTML, CSS, and JavaScript functionalities. In order to learn something new in every chapter, we will use different approaches for the common tasks. For sure, there are things that we need to do every time, for example, running a server that listens on a particular port. JavaScript is a really interesting language, and in most cases, we can solve the same problems in completely different ways. In the previous chapters, we used Express to send assets to the users. In addition, there were examples where we did this directly by reading the files with the filesystem API. However, this time, we will combine the ideas of the two methods, that is, the code that we will use will read the resources from the hard disk and we will work with dynamic paths.

Running the Node.js server

We will start the project in an empty directory. In the beginning, we need an empty `index.js` file that will host the Node.js server. Let's put the following content in the `index.js` file:

```
var http = require('http'),
   fs = require('fs'),
   files = {},
   debug = true,
   port = 3000;
var respond = function(file, res) {
   var contentType;
   switch(file.ext) {
      case "css": contentType = "text/css"; break;
      case "html": contentType = "text/html"; break;
      case "js": contentType = "application/javascript"; break;
      case "ico": contentType = "image/ico"; break;
      default: contentType = "text/plain";
   }
   res.writeHead(200, {'Content-Type': contentType});
   res.end(file.content);
}
var serveAssets = function(req, res) {
   var file = req.url === '/' ? 'html/page.html' : req.url;
   if(!files[file] || debug) {
```

```
    try {
      files[file] = {
        content: fs.readFileSync(__dirname + "/" + file),
        ext: file.split(".").pop().toLowerCase()
      }
    } catch(err) {
      res.writeHead(404, {'Content-Type': 'plain/text'});
      res.end('Missing resource: ' + file);
      return;
    }
  }
  respond(files[file], res);
}
var app = http.createServer(function (req, res) {
  serveAssets(req, res);
}).listen(port, '127.0.0.1');
console.log("Listening on 127.0.0.1:" + port);
```

The script starts with the definition of some global variables. The http module is used to run the Node.js server and fs is run to access the files. The files object acts as a cache for already requested files. Reading the files from the hard disk can be a very expensive operation, so there is really no need to do this in every single request. It's a good practice to cache the content whenever possible. The debug variable is set to true while we are developing the application. This actually turns off our caching mechanisms because otherwise, we need to restart the server every time we make changes to some of the HTML, CSS, or JavaScript files. There is a short respond method, which accepts an object with the following format:

```
{
  content: '...',
  ext: '...'
}
```

The content property is the actual file's content and the ext property represents the file's extension. The same method also needs the response object, so it can send information to the browser. Based on the file's type, we set the proper Content-Type header. This is important because if we skip this, the browser may not process the resource correctly. Next, the serveAssets method gets the current requested path and tries to read the actual file from the system. It also checks whether the file is not in the cache or whether we are in the debug mode. If the file is missing, it sends a 404 error page to the browser. The last lines simply run the server and pass the request and response objects to serveAssets. With this code, we are able to request files with URLs that match their actual directory path.

Managing the to-do lists

We have set up the server, so we can now continue writing the business logic, that is, the logic that will manage the tasks from our to-do list. Let's define the following two new variables at the top of the file:

```
var todos = [],
    ids = 0;
```

The `todos` array will keep our tasks. Every task will be a simple JavaScript object, as shown in the following code:

```
{
    id: <number>,
    text: <string>,
    done: <true | false>
}
```

We will increment the `ids` variable every time we need to add a new to-do activity. So, every object in the array will have a unique ID attached to it. Of course, normally, we will not rely on a single number to identify the different tasks, but the `ids` variable will work for our little experiment. The following is the function that will add a new element to the `todos` array:

```
var addToDo = function(data) {
    data.id = ++ids;
    todos.push(data);
    return data;
}
```

We should have two other methods for deleting and editing a to-do list. They are as follows:

```
var deleteToDo = function(id) {
    var arr = [];
    for(var i=0; i<todos.length; i++) {
        if(todos[i].id !== parseInt(id)) {
            arr.push(todos[i]);
        }
    }
    todos = arr;
    return id;
}
var editToDo = function(id, data) {
    for(var i=0; i<todos.length; i++) {
```

```
      if(todos[i].id === parseInt(id)) {
        todos[i].text = data.text;
        todos[i].done = data.done;
        return todos[i];
      }
    }
}
```

The `deleteToDo` function loops through the elements and skips the one that matches the passed ID. The `editToDo` function is almost the same, except that it updates the properties of the stored object.

We have methods to manage the data; now, we have to write the part that will use them. In general, our server has two roles. The first one is to deliver the usual HTML, CSS, and JavaScript functionalities to the browser. The other one is to act as a REST service, that is, accept the CRUD type of requests and respond to them. Backbone. js will send JSON objects and will expect to receive resources in the same format. So, we have the `respond` function and the following code defines the `respondJSON` function, which will send the data to the browser:

```
var respondJSON = function(json, res) {
  res.writeHead(200, {'Content-Type': 'application/json'});
  res.end(JSON.stringify(json));
}
```

The entry point of our server is the handler of the `http.createServer` method. This is where we need to divide the application's flow, as shown in the following code:

```
var app = http.createServer(function (req, res) {
  if(req.url.indexOf('/api') === 0) {
    serveToDos(req, res);
  } else {
    serveAssets(req, res);
  }
}).listen(port, '127.0.0.1');
```

We will check whether the current URL starts with /api. If not, then we serve the assets. Otherwise, the request is considered as a CRUD operation, as shown in the following code:

```
var serveToDos = function(req, res) {
  if(req.url.indexOf('/api/all') === 0) {
    respondJSON(todos, res);
  } else if(req.url.indexOf('/api/todo') === 0) {
    if(req.method == 'POST') {
```

```
            processPOSTRequest(req, function(data) {
                respondJSON(addToDo(data), res);
            });
        } else if(req.method == 'DELETE') {
            deleteToDo(req.url.split("/").pop());
            respondJSON(todos, res);
        } else if(req.method == 'PUT') {
            processPOSTRequest(req, function(data) {
                respondJSON(editToDo(req.url.split("/").pop(), data),
                    res);
            });
        }
    } else {
        respondJSON({error: 'Missing method'}, res);
    }
}
```

There are two paths that control everything. The `/api/all` path responds with a JSON code that contains all the to-do lists available. The next `/api/todo` path is responsible for creating, editing, and deleting a task. The actual address that is used is `http://localhost:3000/api/todo/4`, where the number at the end is the ID of an element in the `todos` array. That's why we need `req.url.split("/").pop()`, which extracts the number from the URL. There is one additional function called `processPOSTRequest`. It's a helper that gets the data sent via the POST or PUT methods. In Express, the same functionality is provided by the `bodyParser` middleware. The `processPOSTRequest` function is given in the following code:

```
var processPOSTRequest = function(req, callback) {
    var body = '';
    req.on('data', function (data) {
        body += data;
    });
    req.on('end', function () {
        callback(JSON.parse(body));
    });
}
```

At the end, maybe it's a good idea to fill the `todos` array with some tasks. Add the following methods just to have something to display once we build the frontend:

```
addToDo({text: "Learn JavaScript", done: false});
addToDo({text: "Learn Node.js", done: false});
addToDo({text: "Learn BackboneJS", done: false});
```

Writing the frontend

In this section, we will develop the client-side logic — the code that will run in the browser of the users. This includes the listing and managing of the to-do lists delivered by the Node.js part.

Looking into the base of the application

Before we start coding, let's have a look at the file structure. The following figure shows how our project should look:

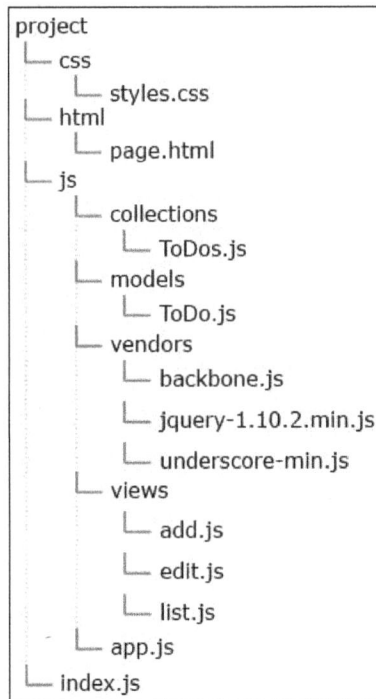

```
project
 └─ css
        └─ styles.css
 └─ html
        └─ page.html
 └─ js
        └─ collections
               └─ ToDos.js
        └─ models
               └─ ToDo.js
        └─ vendors
               └─ backbone.js
               └─ jquery-1.10.2.min.js
               └─ underscore-min.js
        └─ views
               └─ add.js
               └─ edit.js
               └─ list.js
        └─ app.js
 └─ index.js
```

The `index.js` file contains the Node.js code that we already wrote. The `.css` and `.html` directories hold the styles and the HTML markup of the page. In the `.js` folder, we will put the collection, model, and views of Backbone.js. Along with that, there are the framework's dependencies and the main application's `app.js` file. Let's start with the `page.html` file:

```html
<!doctype html>
<html>
  <head>
```

```
        <link rel="stylesheet" type="text/css" href="css/styles.css">
    </head>
    <body>

        <div id="menu">
          <a href="#new">Add new ToDo</a>
          <a href="#">Show all ToDos</a>
        </div>
        <div id="content"></div>

        <script src="js/vendors/jquery-1.10.2.min.js"></script>
        <script src="js/vendors/underscore-min.js"></script>
        <script src="js/vendors/backbone.js"></script>
        <script src="js/app.js"></script>
        <script src="js/models/ToDo.js"></script>
        <script src="js/collections/ToDos.js"></script>
        <script src="js/views/list.js"></script>
        <script src="js/views/add.js"></script>
        <script src="js/views/edit.js"></script>
        <script>
          window.onload = app.init;
        </script>
        </body>
    </html>
```

The styles are added to the `head` tag of the page. The scripts are put at the end, just before closing the `body` tag. We do this because the JavaScript files usually block the rendering of the page. Adding them at the top of the page means that the browser will not get the necessary styles and HTML markup and will not display anything to the user.

We have a menu with two buttons. The first one will show a form where the user can add a new to-do list. The second one shows the home page, that is, a list with all the tasks. The content `div` element will be the host container where we will render Backbone.js's views. The bootstrapping of the application is done in the `init` method of the `app` object as follows:

```
var app = (function() {
  var init = function() { }
  return {
    models: {},
    collections: {},
    views: {},
    init: init
  }
})();
```

We will use the **Revealing Module** pattern. The `app` object has its own private scope. Its public API consists of namespaces for the models, collections, and views. The last thing is the `init` method. It's a good practice to use namespaces. They encapsulate our application and prevent collisions.

The first thing we want to do is to display the current available tasks. Let's write a few things in advance. It is clear that we will put the user interface in the content `div` element. So, it is a good idea to cache a reference to that element because we will use it multiple times. We can define a variable and assign a jQuery object to it as follows:

```
var content;
var init = function() {
   content = $("#content");
}
```

Next, we need a view class that will list the data. However, the view itself should not make requests to the backend. That's the job of the model — `/js/models/ToDo.js`; its code is given as follows:

```
app.models.ToDo = Backbone.Model.extend({
   defaults: {
      text: '',
      done: false
   },
   url: function() {
       return '/api/todo/' + this.get("id");
   }
});
```

We are using the namespace created in `/js/app.js`. Backbone.js offers the `defaults` property, which we may use to define the initial values. Here, the `url` method is very important. Without it, the framework can't send requests to the server. The logic that manages the to-do lists at the backend requires an ID. That's why we need to construct the URL dynamically.

And, of course, we may have a lot of tasks, so we need a `/js/collections/ToDos.js` collection, and its code is given as follows:

```
app.collections.ToDos = Backbone.Collection.extend({
   model: app.models.ToDo,
   url: '/api/all'
});
```

We set up the URL directly as a string. The collection should also know what kind of models are stored in it and we pass the model's class. Keep in mind that we actually extended the classes here. In the following code, we will create an instance of the collection class and call the `fetch` method, which gets the to-do lists stored in the Node.js part:

```
var content,
    todos;
var init = function() {
    content = $("#content");
    todos = new app.collections.ToDos();
    todos.fetch({ success: function() {

    }});
}
```

Our application is useless without the data. We will use the `success` callback and will render the list view once the information arrives.

Before we proceed with the code of the `/js/views/list.js` file, we will clarify a few things about the Backbone.js's views. We mentioned in the beginning of the chapter that there is a DOM element that is automatically created for us. It's available as a `.el` property of the view. There are a few common tasks that we will probably do. The first one is binding DOM events to functions inside the view class. This can happen by applying a value to the `events` property, as shown in the following code:

```
events: {
  'click #delete': 'deleteToDo',
  'click #edit': 'editToDo',
  'click #change-status': 'changeStatus'
}
```

We start with the type of the event followed by an element selector. The value is a function of the view. A big advantage of this technique for event handling is that the `this` keyword in the handler points to the right place, that is, the view. We may need to call `delegateEvents` to reassign the listeners. This is needed when we update the HTML code of the view's DOM element.

The other interesting thing regarding Backbone.js's views is the `render` method. What we normally do there is update the content of the `.el` object. We can use any code we like, but it is good practice to avoid placing HTML tags. That's the function where most developers use a template engine. In our example, we will use the Underscore.js template. It accepts a string and an object with data. As we don't want to place the HTML as a string inside the view, we will add it to the `page.html` file. The markup will be placed inside a script tag, so it doesn't mess up the rest of the valid HTML code. The good news is that we could still get it via jQuery by simply querying the tag. For example, the following is the template used in `/js/views/list.js`:

```
<script type="text/template" id="tpl-list-item">
  <li data-index="<%= index %>" class="<%= done %>">
    <span><%= index+1 %>. <%= text %></span>
    <a href="#edit/<%= index %>" id="edit">edit</a>
    <a href="javascript:void(0);" id="change-status"><%=
      statusLabel %></a>
     <a href="javascript:void(0);" id="delete">delete</a>
  </li>
</script>
```

There are data placeholders for the item's index, text, and status. We will replace them with actual values during the rendering.

Listing the to-do activities

Let's continue with the code of the list view. The one that will show the current added to-do activity is as follows:

```
app.views.list = Backbone.View.extend({
  events: {
    'click #delete': 'deleteToDo',
    'click #change-status': 'changeStatus'
  },
  getIndex: function(e) {
    return parseInt(e.target.parentNode.getAttribute("data-
      index"));
  },
  deleteToDo: function(e) {
    this.model.at(this.getIndex(e)).destroy();
    this.render();
  },
  changeStatus: function(e) {
    var self = this;
```

```
        var model = this.model.at(this.getIndex(e));
        model.save({ done: !model.get("done") }, {
          wait: true,
          success: function() {
            self.render()
          }
        });
      },
      render: function() {
        var html = '<ul class="list">',
        self = this;
        this.model.each(function(todo, index) {
        var template = _.template($("#tpl-list-item").html());
        html += template({
          text: todo.get("text"),
            index: index,
            done: todo.get("done") ? "done" : "not-done",
            statusLabel: todo.get("done") ? "mark as not done" : "mark
              as done"
          });
        });
        html += '</ul>';
        this.$el.html(html);
        this.delegateEvents();
        return this;
      }
    });
```

We define the view class in the correct namespace. We will pass the collection of to-do activities as a model, so the this.model statement will give us an access to all the tasks. In the render method, we loop through every model and construct an unordered list, which is at the end and appended to the DOM element. We are using $el instead of el because our project has jQuery included, and Backbone.js automatically starts working with it. Note that we are sending different values of done and statusLabel based on the status of the task. If we check the preceding template, we will see that done is actually a CSS class. Applying a different class will allow us to distinguish the items in the list. We should not forget to run the delegateEvents method at the end. We are updating the children elements of $el, so every event listener that is attached is removed.

In the beginning of the class, we define two events. The first one deletes a to-do activity from the system. Backbone.js has a destroy method for such cases. However, to reach the exact model from the collection, we need its index (ID). If we check the HTML template, will see that every `li` tag has a `data-index` attribute that contains exactly what we need. That's what the `getIndex` helper does—it gets the value of that attribute. Similarly, `changeStatus` updates the `done` field of the to-do lists. After every modification, we call the `render` method. This is quite important for the users because they have to see that the change is done.

Now, let's change the `app.js` file a bit and render the view, as shown in the following code:

```
var content,
   todos;
var showList = function() {
   content.empty().append(list.render().$el);
}
var init = function() {
   content = $("#content");
   todos = new app.collections.ToDos();
   list = new app.views.list({model: todos});
   todos.fetch({ success: function() {
     showList();
   }});
}
```

There is one new method, `showList`, which triggers the rendering of the view and appends its DOM element to the content `div` element. Now, if we run the application by typing `node ./index.js` in our console, we will see the three to-do activities, which we added, being displayed on the screen.

Adding, deleting, and editing the to-do lists

The next logical step is to develop the code for the adding, editing, and deleting of tasks. So, we need two new pages, additional logic to show the two new views, and a few lines that will remove tasks. We will also need a router that will handle the new content. To simplify the process, let's directly see how the final `/js/app.js` file looks:

```
var app = (function() {
   var todos, content, list, add, edit, router;
   var showList = function() {
     content.empty().append(list.render().$el);
   }
```

```javascript
    var showNewToDoForm = function() {
      content.empty().append(add.$el);
      add.delegateEvents();
    }
    var showEditToDoForm = function(data) {
      content.empty().append(edit.render(data).$el);
    }
    var home = function() {
      router.navigate("", {trigger: true});
    }
    var RouterClass = Backbone.Router.extend({
      routes: {
        "new": "newToDo",
        "edit/:index": "editToDo",
        "": "list"
      },
      list: showList,
      newToDo: showNewToDoForm,
      editToDo: function(index) {
        showEditToDoForm({ index: index });
      }
    });
    var init = function() {
      todos = new app.collections.ToDos();
      list = new app.views.list({model: todos});
      edit = (new app.views.edit({model: todos}));
      add = (new app.views.add({model: todos})).render();
      content = $("#content");
      todos.fetch({ success: function() {
        router = new RouterClass();
        Backbone.history.start();
      }});
      add.on("saved", home);
      edit.on("edited", home);
    }
    return {
      models: {},
      collections: {},
      views: {},
      init: init
    }
})();
```

We have put a few new variables at the top. The add and edit variables represent the two new views. There are two new functions that change the content div element. Note that we are not calling the render method of the add view. This is because there is nothing dynamic in it, which means that there is no need to render it repeatedly. It's just a form that submits data. The showEditToDoForm function is almost the same as the showList function, except that we expect one additional parameter — data. This should be an object with a format {index: <number>}. Once we have the index of the to-do list, we can easily get its fields. We will need these fields because we have to fill the form for editing.

Next, the home method simply uses the navigate method of the router and returns the user to the list view. The next thing in the script is the definition of the router. The described paths call the functions that we just went through. It's the mapping of URL addresses to JavaScript functions.

There are quite a few new things inside the init method, so let's have a closer look. The two new views, add and edit, are initialized, and again they accept the collection's to-do activities. We will also start listening for two events. The views dispatch the saved event when a new to-do activity is added and the edited event when some of the tasks are updated.

The view for adding new tasks is as follows:

```
app.views.add = Backbone.View.extend({
  events: {
    "click button": "save"
  },
  save: function() {
    var textarea = this.$el.find("textarea");
    var value = textarea.val();
    if(value != "") {
      var self = this;
      this.model.create({ text: value }, {
        wait: true,
        success: function() {
          textarea.val("");
          self.trigger("saved");
        }
      });
    } else {
      alert("Please, type something.");
    }
  },
  render: function() {
```

```
        var template = _.template($("#tpl-todo").html());
        this.$el.html(template());
        this.delegateEvents();
         return this;
      }
  });
```

There is validation of the user's input. If there is text entered in the textarea element, we call the create method of the collection that initializes a new model. It also sends a POST request to the server. Once the operation finishes, we empty the textbox and trigger the saved event so that the code in /js/app.js can forward the user to the home page. The views for adding and editing need a separate template. The following is the code of that template:

```
<script type="text/template" id="tpl-todo">
  <div class="form">
    <textarea></textarea>
      <button>save</button>
  </div>
</script>
```

The /js/views/edit.js file has almost the same code, which is given as follows:

```
app.views.edit = Backbone.View.extend({
  events: {
    'click button': 'save'
  },
  save: function() {
    var textarea = this.$el.find('textarea');
    var value = textarea.val();
    if(value != '') {
      var self = this;
      this.selectedModel.save({text: value}, {
      wait: true,
      success: function() {
        self.trigger('edited');
      }
    });
    } else {
      alert('Please, type something.');
    }
  },
  render: function(data) {
    this.selectedModel = this.model.at(data.index);
```

```
        var template = _.template($('#tpl-todo').html());
        this.$el.html(template());
        this.$el.find('textarea').val(this.selectedModel.get('text'));
        this.delegateEvents();
        return this;
    }
});
```

The difference is that it puts a value in the `textarea` element and calls the `save` method of the edited model instead of the `create` function of the whole collection.

Summary

In this chapter, we learned how to work with Backbone.js. We used a model, collection, router, and several views to implement a simple to-do application. Thankfully, due to the event-driven nature of the framework, we bound everything together. Node.js took an interesting and important part in this small project. It handled the requests from the client-side's JavaScript and acted as a REST service.

The next chapter is dedicated to command-line programming. We will see how to use Node.js from the command line and will develop a script that uploads our photos to Flickr.

6
Using Node.js as a Command-line Tool

In the previous chapters, we learned how to use Node.js with client-side frameworks, such as AngularJS and Backbone.js. Each time, we ran the backend from the command line. Node.js is suitable not only for web applications, but also for developing command-line tools. The access to the filesystem, the various built-in modules, and the great community makes Node.js an attractive environment for such kind of programs.

In this chapter, we will detail the process of developing a command-line tool to upload pictures on **Flickr**. By the end of this chapter, we will have created a program that finds images in a particular directory and uploads them on Internet portals.

Exploring the required modules

We will use several modules to make our life easier, which are listed as follows:

- `fs`: This gives us access to the filesystem, and is a built-in feature of the Node.js module.

- `optimist`: This is a module that parses the parameters passed to our Node.js script.

- `readline`: This allows the reading of a stream (such as `process.stdin`) on a line-by-line basis. We will use it for getting input from the user while our application is still running. The module is added in Node.js by default.

- `glob`: This module reads a directory and returns all the existing files that match a predefined specific pattern.

- open: At some point, we will need to open a page in the user's default browser. Node.js runs on different operating systems that have different commands to open the default browser. This module helps us by providing one API.

- flapi: This is the Flickr API wrapper used to communicate with Flickr's services.

Based on the preceding list, we can write and use the following package.json file:

```
{
  "name": "FlickrUploader",
  "description": "Command line tool",
  "version": "0.0.1",
  "dependencies": {
    "flapi": "*",
    "open": "*",
    "optimist": "*",
    "glob": "*"
  },
  "main": "index.js",
  "bin": {
    "flickruploader": "./index.js"
  }
}
```

The entry point of our script is the index.js file. Thus, we set it as a value of the main property. There is another feature which we haven't used so far—the bin property. This is the key/pair mapping of the binary script names and the Node.js script paths. In other words, when our module is published in the Node.js package manager's register and later installed, our console will automatically have the flickruploader command available. During the installation, the npm command checks whether we have passed something to the bin property. If yes, then it creates our script's symlink. It is also important that we add the #!/usr/bin/env node at the top of our index.js file. This is how the system will know that the script should be processed with Node.js. At the end, if we type the command and press *Enter*, our script will be run.

Planning the application

We can split the command-line tool into two parts: the first one reads a directory and returns all the files in it and the second one sends the images to Flickr. It's a good idea to form these two functionalities in different modules. The following diagram shows how our project will appear:

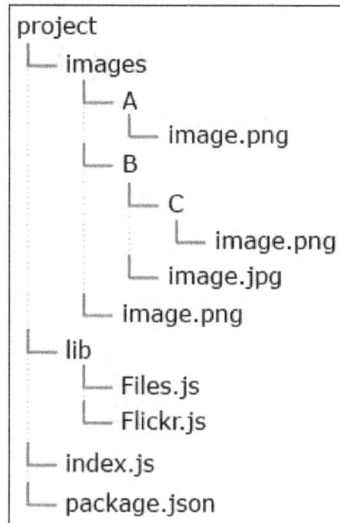

```
project
 └─ images
       └─ A
             └─ image.png
       └─ B
             └─ C
                   └─ image.png
             └─ image.jpg
       └─ image.png
 └─ lib
       └─ Files.js
       └─ Flickr.js
 └─ index.js
 └─ package.json
```

The `images` directory will be used as a test folder, that is, our script will do its job in that directory. Of course, we can have another one if we want. The two modules mentioned previously are saved in the `lib` directory. So, we should first get the files (`Files.js`) and then upload them (`Flickr.js`) to the portal. The two operations are asynchronous, so both the modules should accept **callbacks**. The following is the content of the `index.js` file:

```
var flickr = require('./lib/Flickr');
var files = require('./lib/Files');
var flickrOptions = {};

files(function(images) {
  flickr(flickrOptions, images, function() {
    console.log("All the images uploaded.");
    process.exit(1);
  })
});
```

The `Files` module will look into the specified folder and scan it for subfolders and images. All the files that are pictures are returned as a parameter of the passed callback. These pictures are sent to the `Flickr` module. Along with the files, we will also pass few settings needed to access Flickr's services. Eventually, once everything goes well, we will call `process.exit(1)` to terminate the program and return the user to the terminal.

Obtaining images from a folder

The `Files.js` file starts with the definition of the required modules:

```
var fs = require('fs');
var argv = require('optimist').argv;
var readline = require('readline');
var glob = require('glob');
```

Immediately after, we need to define two variables. The `currentDirectory` variable stores the path to the current working directory and `rl` is an instance of the `readline` module.

```
var currentDirectory = process.cwd() + '/';
var rl = readline.createInterface({
  input: process.stdin,
  output: process.stdout
});
```

The `createInterface` function accepts an object. The two required fields are `input` and `output`. The `input` field will point to the incoming readable stream and `output` to the writable stream. In our case, the user will type data directly into the terminal/console, so we will pass `process.stdin`.

At the beginning of the chapter, we mentioned the `optimist` module. We will use it to get the parameter from the command line. In our case, this will be the directory used to parse. It's always good to provide an alternative way to apply settings, that is, in addition to asking the user, accept a command-line argument. Every Node.js script has a global object, `process`, which has the `argv` property. This property is an array of arguments passed from the terminal. The `optimist` module simplifies the parsing and provides an effective API to access these arguments.

Let's add the following code immediately after the definition of the `rl` variable:

```
module.exports = function(callback) {
  if(argv.s) {
    readDirectory(currentDirectory + argv.s, callback);
  } else {
    getPath(function(path) {
      readDirectory(path, callback);
    });
  }
};
```

When navigating to the project's directory to run our Node.js program, type `node ./index.js`. This will run the script without arguments and will ask the user for the folder that contains the pictures. However, we can also pass this information at an early stage directly from the terminal by running `node ./index.js -s images`. In the previous code snippet, `argv.s` will be equal to `images`. So, we should check whether such a parameter is passed, and if yes, we continue with searching the image files. If not, ask the user via the `readline` module, the `getPath` function, as in the following code:

```
var getPath = function(callback) {
  rl.question('Please type a path to directory: ', function(answer) {
    callback(currentDirectory + answer);
  });
}
```

The callback of the question method returns the text typed by the user. All we have to do is pass it to the `readDirectory` function, as follows:

```
var readDirectory = function(path, callback) {
  if(fs.existsSync(path)) {
    glob(path + "/**/*.+(jpg|jpeg|gif|png)", function(err, files)
    {
      if(err) {
        throw new Error('Can\'t read the directory.');
      }
      console.log("Found images:");
      files.forEach(function(file) {
        console.log(file.replace(/\//g, '\\').replace(process.cwd(),
''));
      });
```

```
        rl.question('Are you sure (y/n)? ', function(answer) {
          if(answer == 'y') {
            callback(files);
          }
          rl.close();
        });
      });
    } else {
      getPath(function(path) {
        readDirectory(path, callback);
        });
    }
  }
```

Of course, we should check whether the path is valid. For this, we will use the `fs.existsSync` method. If the directory exists, we get the files that match the following pattern:

```
/**/*.+(jpg|jpeg|gif|png)
```

This means parse the directory and all its subdirectories and search for the files ending with `jpg`, `jpeg`, `gif`, or `png`. The `glob` module helps a lot in such cases.

Before sending the files back to `index.js`, we display them and ask the user for a confirmation. This is again done with the `readline` module included at the beginning. It is important to use `rl.close()`. This method relinquishes the control over the input and output streams.

Authorizing the Flickr protocol

We will use the `flapi` module to communicate with Flickr. It provides access to the API methods. Most large-scale companies implement some level of authorization. In other words, we can't just make a request and upload/retrieve data. We need to sign in our requests with access tokens or provide credentials during the process. Flickr uses **OAuth** (1.0 specification), a type of standard for such operations. OAuth is an open standard for authorization and defines a method for clients to access server resources. Let's check the following diagram and see how Flickr's OAuth mechanism works:

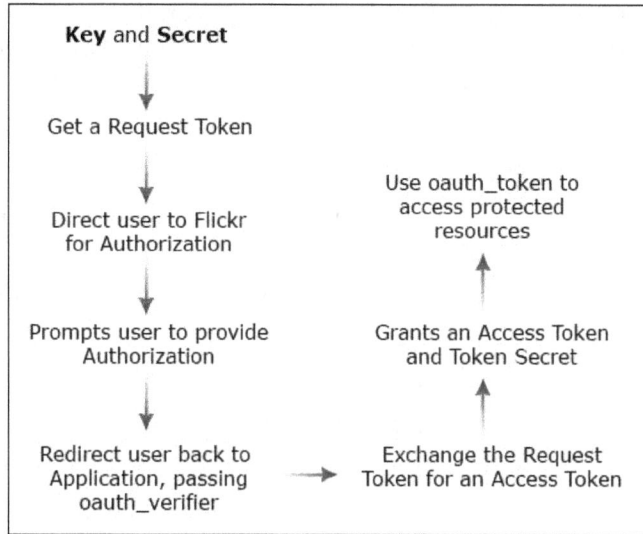

Almost the entire process is wrapped in the `flapi` module. What we should remember here is that we need a **Key** and **Secret** to retrieve an access token. The same token will be used later when uploading the images.

Obtaining your application's Key and Secret

To create our own application's *Key* and *Secret*, we must have a valid Flickr account first. Next, log in and navigate to `http://www.flickr.com/services/apps/create/apply/`. On this page, click on **APPLY FOR A NON-COMMERCIAL KEY**, which is the blue button.

We are building a non-commercial application; however, if you plan to use the key for commercial purposes, go with the second option on the right. After that, you will see a form with few fields. Fill them and click on the **SUBMIT** button, as shown in the following screenshot:

Tell us about your app:

Owner

KrasimirTsonev

This app will be associated with your **KrasimirTsonev** account. You will not be able to change this after you submit your application.

What's the name of your app?

Node.js command line tool

What are you building?

(And trust us when we say you can't be detailed enough)

A command line tool which uploads images.

☑ I acknowledge that Flickr members own all rights to their content, and that it's my responsibility to make sure that my project does not contravene those rights.

☑ I agree to comply with the Flickr API Terms of Use.

SUBMIT or Cancel

The next screen, which will be shown, contains our **Key** and **Secret**. It should look like the following screenshot:

The App Garden

Create an App   API Documentation   Feeds   What is the App Garden?

Done! Here's the API key and secret for your new app:

Node.js command line tool

Key:
78ab5d81a61f6bd75417527bfed4b163

Secret:
2c0bc847c2daedd1

Edit app details · Edit auth flow for this app · View all Apps by You

Writing into the Flickr.js module

Once we get the **Key** and **Secret** values, we can continue and start writing our lib/
Flickr.js module. Here is the initial code of the file:

```
var open = require('open');
var http = require('http');
var url = require('url');
var Flapi = require('flapi');

var flapiClient;
var filesToOpen;
var done;
var options;

module.exports = function(opts, files, callback) {
  options = opts;
  filesToOpen = files;
  done = callback;
  createFlapiClient();
}
```

The required dependencies are at the beginning of the previous code. We mentioned
the open module; here, http is used to run a Node.js HTTP server and url is used
to parse parameters from an incoming request. The module exports a function that
accepts three arguments. The first one contains the Flickr's API settings such as **Key**
and **Secret**. The second argument is an array of the files that need to be uploaded. At
the end, we accept a callback function, which will be called once the uploading is
complete. We save everything in a few global variables and call createFlapiClient,
which will initialize the flapi object. Before we see what exactly happens in
createFlapiClient, let's edit index.js and pass the needed options, as follows:

```
var flickr = require('./lib/Flickr');
var files = require('./lib/Files');
var flickrOptions = {
  oauth_consumer_key: "ebce9c7a68eb009f8db5bcc41d139320",
  oauth_consumer_secret: "a9277a76c947c0b3",
    // oauth_token: '',
    // oauth_token_secret: '',
  perms: 'write'
};
```

We left flickrOptions empty, but now is the time to fill it. Set **Key** as the value of oauth_consumer_key and **Secret** as the value of oauth_consumer_secret. The tokens oauth_token and oauth_token_secret are commented by default, but once we perform the initial authorizing, we will set their values. At the end, there is also a permissions property, which should be set to write because we will upload the photos.

When the right options are configured in Flickr.js, we can create our flapi client and start querying Flickr's servers, as shown in the following code:

```
var createFlapiClient = function(){
  flapiClient = new Flapi(options);
  if(!options.oauth_token) {
    flapiClient.authApp('http://127.0.0.1:3000',
function(oauthResults){
      runServer(function() {
        open(flapiClient.getUserAuthURL());
      })
    });
  } else {
    uploadPhotos();
  }
};
```

We pass the settings, currently oauth_consumer_key, oauth_consumer_secret, and perms. Note that oauth_token is undefined and we need to authorize our application. This happens in the browser. The mechanism defined by Flickr requires the opening of a specific URL and the passing of a callback address, where the user will be redirected to after being granted the permissions. We are developing a command-line tool, so we can't really provide that address because our script is in the terminal. Therefore, we run our own HTTP server, which will accept requests from Flickr. Of course, this server will be available only on our machine and during the script execution. But that should be enough because we need it only during the first time. If everything goes well, we will get the oauth_token and oauth_token_secret values, as shown in the following code. We will set them in flickrOptions and the HTTP server will not be run next time. When the server is started, we open a new page in the user's default browser, passing the correct URL returned by flapiClient.getUserAuthURL.

The code underlying runServer is as follows:

```
var runServer = function(callback) {
    http.createServer(function (req, res) {
    res.writeHead(200, {'Content-Type': 'text/html'});
```

```
        var urlParts = url.parse(req.url, true);
        var query = urlParts.query;
        if(query.oauth_token) {
        flapiClient.getUserAccessToken(query.oauth_verifier,
function(result) {
            options.oauth_token = result.oauth_token;
            options.oauth_token_secret = result.oauth_token_secret;
            var message = '';
            for(var prop in result) {
               message += prop + ' = ' + result[prop] + '<br />';
            }
            res.end(message);
            uploadPhotos();
        });
        } else {
            res.end('Missing oauth_token parameter.');
        }
    }).listen(3000, '127.0.0.1');
    console.log('Server running at http://127.0.0.1:3000/');
    callback();
}
```

The server listens on port 3000, and it has only one handler. The request we are waiting for contains the *GET* parameter oauth_verifier. We will get access to it by using the url module and its parse method. It's also important that we send true as the second parameter so that Node.js parses the query string of the request. By passing oauth_verifier to flapi, the client's getUserAccessToken method, we will get the needed token and secret. There is an uploadPhotos function called at the end, but we will leave its body empty for now. This will be filled in the next section of the chapter.

Running our application tool

Now, let's run our tool. Type node ./index.js into your terminal and you will see what is shown in the following screenshot:

```
Please type a path to directory:
```

Our test directory is images, so we type this string and click on *Enter*. The code in Files.js will scan the directory for images and will ask us for a confirmation, as shown in the following screenshot:

```
Please type a path to directory: images
Found images:
\images\A\image.png
\images\B\C\image.png
\images\B\image.jpg
\images\image.png
Are you sure (y/n)? _
```

Type **y** and press *Enter*. A message will be displayed that the server is running and a new page will open in our default browser. It will ask us to grant the application permission to perform several actions, as shown in the following screenshot:

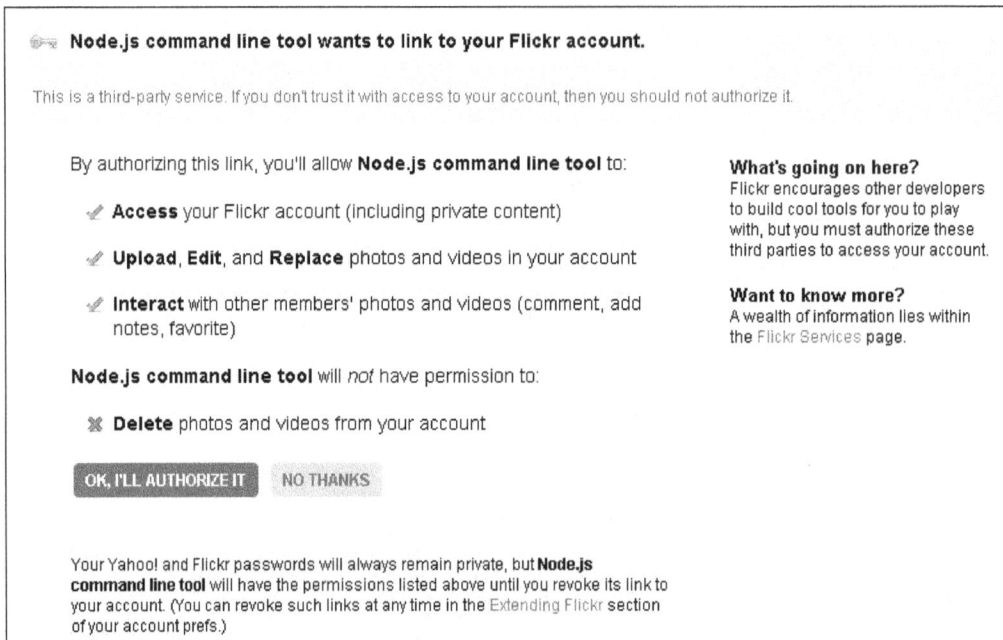

Node.js command line tool wants to link to your Flickr account.

This is a third-party service. If you don't trust it with access to your account, then you should not authorize it.

By authorizing this link, you'll allow **Node.js command line tool** to:

- **Access** your Flickr account (including private content)

- **Upload**, **Edit**, and **Replace** photos and videos in your account

- **Interact** with other members' photos and videos (comment, add notes, favorite)

Node.js command line tool will *not* have permission to:

- **Delete** photos and videos from your account

OK, I'LL AUTHORIZE IT   **NO THANKS**

Your Yahoo! and Flickr passwords will always remain private, but **Node.js command line tool** will have the permissions listed above until you revoke its link to your account. (You can revoke such links at any time in the Extending Flickr section of your account prefs.)

What's going on here?
Flickr encourages other developers to build cool tools for you to play with, but you must authorize these third parties to access your account.

Want to know more?
A wealth of information lies within the Flickr Services page.

Click on the blue button with text **OK, I'LL AUTHORIZE IT**. There are two things happening at the moment. The browser sends a request with the oauth_ verifier parameter to our Node.js server. We use the value, pass it to the getUserAccessToken method, and fetch the needed oauth_token and oauth_ token_secret values. At the same time, the browser gets a response, and we see something similar to the following screenshot:

```
fullname = Krasimir Tsonev
oauth_token = 72157639968574353-895de370c5997f98
oauth_token_secret = 4eba51016cab81fa
user_nsid = 114621618@N06
username = KrasimirTsonev
```

We will get the information from the second and third lines and put it in the
flickrOptions object, which is initialized in the index.js file. By doing this, we
will avoid the steps performed with the Node.js server next time. The script will be
able to upload the photos directly without asking for the token and secret.

Uploading the images

The last function that we will write is the uploadPhotos method for the Flickr.js
module. It will use the global filesToOpen array and upload the files one by one.
Since the operation is asynchronous, we will continuously execute the function till
the array is empty. We can see the code for this as follows:

```
var uploadPhotos = function() {
  if(filesToOpen.length === 0) {
    done();
  } else {
    var file = filesToOpen.shift();
    console.log("Uploading " + file.replace(/\//g, '\\').
replace(process.cwd(), ''));
    flapiClient.api({
      method: 'upload',
      params:  { photo : file },
      accessToken : {
        oauth_token: options.oauth_token,
        oauth_token_secret: options.oauth_token_secret
      },
      next: function(data){
          uploadPhotos();
      }
    });
  }
}
```

The done callback returns the application flow to index.js, where the script is terminated. The result of the entire process will look like the following screenshot:

```
Please type a path to directory: images
Found images:
\images\A\image.png
\images\B\C\image.png
\images\B\image.jpg
\images\image.png
Are you sure (y/n)? y
Server running at http://127.0.0.1:3000/
Uploading \images\A\image.png
Uploading \images\B\C\image.png
Uploading \images\B\image.jpg
Uploading \images\image.png
All the images uploaded.
```

Summary

In this chapter, we learned how to use Node.js as a command-line tool. We successfully got arguments from the terminal, searched directories for image files, and uploaded them to Flickr. Most of the raw operations such as access to the filesystem or the Flickr OAuth implementation were delegated to different modules, which we added as dependencies to the project. More and more instruments are emerging everyday which transform Node.js into an attractive environment to develop not only web-based applications, but also command-line scripts.

In the next chapter, we will learn how to use Node.js and Ember.js together. We will get a Twitter social feed and display it on the browser.

7
Showing a Social Feed with Ember.js

In the previous chapter, we learned how to create a command-line tool that uploads photos to Flickr. In this chapter, we will communicate with one of the most popular social networks: **Twitter**. We will create an application that gets the latest tweets based on a user handle and shows them on the screen. Node.js will be responsible for the communication with the Twitter API, and Ember.js will take care of the user interface. The following is a short list of the topics that we will cover in this chapter:

- Introduction to the Ember.js framework
- Communicating with Twitter's API
- Wiring Node.js with Ember.js to obtain tweets

Preparing the application

We have worked on applications in the previous chapters. For this application, we need a Node.js server, which will deliver the necessary HTML, CSS, and JavaScript code. The following is the package.json file, which we are starting from:

```
{
  "name": "TwitterFeedShower",
  "description": "Show Twitter feed",
  "version": "0.0.1",
  "dependencies": {
    "twit": "*"
  },
  "main": "index.js"
}
```

There is only one dependency and that's the module that will connect to Twitter. After you run `npm install` in the same folder as the `package.json` file, the module will appear in the newly created `node_modules` directory.

The next step is to create the folders for the HTML, CSS, and JavaScript and put the necessary files inside these folders. In addition, create the main `index.js` file that will contain the code of our Node.js server. At the end, our project directory should look like the following diagram:

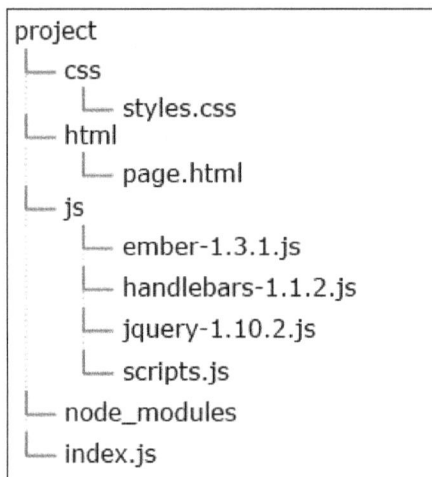

```
project
  └─ css
         └─ styles.css
  └─ html
         └─ page.html
  └─ js
         └─ ember-1.3.1.js
         └─ handlebars-1.1.2.js
         └─ jquery-1.10.2.js
         └─ scripts.js
  └─ node_modules
  └─ index.js
```

The CSS styles of the project will go to `css/styles.css`. The templates will be placed in the `html/page.html` file and the custom JavaScript code will be written to `js/scripts.js`. The other `.js` files are Ember.js itself and its two dependencies: jQuery and Handlebars.

Running the server and delivering the assets

In *Chapter 5, Creating a To-Do Application with Backbone.js*, we built an application with Backbone.js, and we used two helper functions: `serveAssets` and `respond`. The purpose of these functions was to read our HTML, CSS, and JavaScript files and send them as a response to the browser. We will use them again here.

Let's first start by defining the global variables, as follows:

```
var http = require('http'),
    fs = require('fs'),
    port = 3000,
    files = [],
    debug = true;
```

The `http` module provides methods to create and run the Node.js server, and the `fs` module is responsible for reading the files from the filesystem. We are going to listen on port 3000 and the `files` variable will cache the content of the read files. When `debug` is set to `true`, the assets will be read on every request. If it is `false`, their content will be fetched only the first time, but every future response will contain the same code. We are doing this because while we are developing the application, we don't want to stop and run our server just to see the changes in the HTML script. Reading the file on every request guarantees that we are seeing the latest version. However, this is considered as a bad practice when we run the application in a production environment.

Let's continue and run the server using the following code:

```
var app = http.createServer(function (req, res) {
    if(req.url.indexOf("/tweets/") === 0) {
        // ... getting tweets
    } else {
        serveAssets(req, res);
    }
}).listen(port, '127.0.0.1');
console.log("Server listening on port " + port);
```

The callback function, which we passed to `http.createServer`, accepts two arguments: the `request` and `response` objects. The Node.js part of our application will be responsible for two things. The first one is to provide the necessary HTML, CSS, and JavaScript, and the second one is to fetch tweets from Twitter. So, we are checking whether the URL starts with `/tweets` and if it does, then we will process the request differently. Otherwise, `serveAssets` will be called as follows:

```
var serveAssets = function(req, res) {
    var file = req.url === '/' ? 'html/page.html' : req.url;
    if(!files[file] || debug) {
        try {
            files[file] = {
                content: fs.readFileSync(__dirname + "/" + file),
```

```
      ext: file.split(".").pop().toLowerCase()
    }
  } catch(err) {
    res.writeHead(404, {'Content-Type': 'plain/text'});
    res.end('Missing resource: ' + file);
    return;
  }
}
respond(files[file], res);
}
```

In this function, we are getting the requested file path, and we will read the file from the filesystem. Along with the content of the file, we will also get its extension, which is needed to set the response header properly. This is done in the `respond` method, as follows:

```
var respond = function(file, res) {
  var contentType;
  switch(file.ext) {
    case "css": contentType = "text/css"; break;
    case "html": contentType = "text/html"; break;
    case "js": contentType = "application/javascript"; break;
    case "ico": contentType = "image/ico"; break;
    default: contentType = "text/plain";
  }
  res.writeHead(200, {'Content-Type': contentType});
  res.end(file.content);
}
```

This is important because if we don't provide `Content-Type`, the browser may not interpret the response correctly.

And that's everything about the serving of the assets. Let's continue and get information from Twitter.

Getting tweets based on a user handle

Before we write the code that requests data from the Twitter's API, we need to register a new Twitter application. First, we should open `https://dev.twitter.com/` and log in with our Twitter **Name** and **Password**. After that, we need to load `https://dev.twitter.com/apps/new` and fill in the form. It should look like the following screenshot:

Create an application

Application Details

Name: *

NodejsSocialFeed

Your application name. This is used to attribute the source of a tweet and in user-facing authorization screens. 32 characters max.

Description: *

Getting latest tweets

Your application description, which will be shown in user-facing authorization screens. Between 10 and 200 characters max.

Website: *

http://site.com

Your application's publicly accessible home page, where users can go to download, make use of, or find out more information about your application. This fully-qualified URL is used in the source attribution for tweets created by your application and will be shown in user-facing authorization screens.
(If you don't have a URL yet, just put a placeholder here but remember to change it later.)

Callback URL:

Where should we return after successfully authenticating? For @Anywhere applications, only the domain specified in the callback will be used. OAuth 1.0a applications should explicitly specify their `oauth_callback` URL on the request token step, regardless of the value given here. To restrict your application from using callbacks, leave this field blank.

We can leave the **Callback URL** field empty. The **Website** field can have the address of our personal or company site. We should accept the terms and conditions present below the form, and click on **Create your Twitter application**. The next page, which we will see, should be similar to the following screenshot:

The information that we need is located in the third tab: **API Keys**. Once we click on it, Twitter will show us the **API key** and **API secret** fields, as shown in the following screenshot:

NodejsSocialFeed   Test OAuth

Details   Settings   API Keys   Permissions

Application settings

Keep the "API secret" a secret. This key should never be human-readable in your application.

API key	4v8nlz6Jdlp7P3HgkA39hzoU2
API secret	IM0GBz1gwKr5KuywnUbjnWVzXY1VV2pY9uEqhtZ2Oz1Qkzdu5B
Access level	Read-only (modify app permissions)
Owner	KrasimirTsonev
Owner ID	130462642

Application actions

Regenerate API keys   Change App Permissions

Your access token

You haven't authorized this application for your own account yet.

By creating your access token here, you will have everything you need to make API calls right away. The access token generated will be assigned your application's current permission level.

Token actions

Create my access token

Additionally, we will generate an access token and access secret by clicking on the **Create my access token** button. Normally, the data doesn't show up immediately. So, we should wait a bit and refresh the page, if necessary. The resulted document should look like on the following screenshot:

Your access token

This access token can be used to make API requests on your own account's behalf. Do not share your access token secret with anyone.

Access token	130462642-7M3dow5fB0wDTN0bzn7KdiGo2EJBasK6gDkcklEi
Access token secret	16VlHNzfwcjtC6OkAXKvxuPRCerjMAlNoyxGs0sPh3mDd
Access level	Read-only
Owner	KrasimirTsonev
Owner ID	130462642

Token actions

Regenerate my access token   Revoke token access

We will copy the **Access token** and **Access token secret** values. It's a good practice to keep such sensitive information out of the application's code because our program may be transferred from one place to another. Placing the data in an externally configured file will do the job in most cases.

Once we have these four strings, we are able to communicate with Twitter's API. The following variables go at the top of our `index.js` file:

```
var Twit = require('twit');
var T = new Twit({
  consumer_key: '...',
  consumer_secret: '...',
  access_token: '...',
  access_token_secret: '...'
});
var numOfTweets = 10;
```

The `T` variable is actually a Twitter client, which we will use to request the data. We left a place in our server to query the Twitter's API. Let's now put the necessary code in the `index.js` file, which can be seen as follows:

```
var app = http.createServer(function (req, res) {
  if (req.url.indexOf("/tweets/") === 0) {
    var handle = req.url.replace("/tweets/", "");
    T.get("statuses/user_timeline", { screen_name: handle, count:
numOfTweets }, function(err, reply) {
      res.writeHead(200, {'Content-Type': 'application/json'});
      res.end(JSON.stringify(reply));
    });
  } else {
    serveAssets(req, res);
  }
}).listen(port, '127.0.0.1');
```

The request that we need to perform is `http://localhost:3000/tweets/KrasimirTsonev`. The last part of the URL is the Twitter handle of the user. So, the `if` statement becomes `true` because the address starts with `/tweets/`. We extract the username in a variable called `handle`. After that, this variable is sent to the `statuses/user_timeline` resource of the Twitter's API. The result of the request is directly sent to the browser via a stringified JSON.

On a concluding note, the Node.js part of our project provides all the HTML, CSS, and JavaScript code. Along with that, it accepts a Twitter handle and returns the most recent tweets of the user.

Discovering Ember.js

Ember.js is one of the most popular client-side JavaScript frameworks today. It has a great community and its features are well-documented. Ember.js gathers an increasing number of fans because of its architecture. The library uses the Model-View-Controller design pattern, which makes it easy to understand because that pattern is widely used in almost every programming language. It also collaborates well with the REST APIs (we are going to build such an API in *Chapter 11, Writing a REST API*) and eliminates the task of writing the boilerplate code.

Knowing the dependencies of Ember.js

The Ember.js framework has the following two dependencies:

* **jQuery**
* **Handlebars**

The first one is the most used JavaScript tool on the Web today. It provides methods to select and manipulate the DOM elements and a lot of helper functions such as `forEach` or `map`, which help us to work faster. The library also solves some **cross-browser** issues by providing only one API. Like, for example, if we want to attach an event listener to an element, we need to use `attachEvent` in Internet Explorer but `addEventListener` in the other browsers. The simple `.on` method is provided by jQuery, which wraps this functionality. It checks for the current browser and calls the correct function. Along with all these things, we are able to use the `.get` or `.post` functions, which perform AJAX requests.

Handlebars is a template engine library. It extends the HTML syntax by adding expressions and custom tags. It's similar to **Jade**, another template language which we used in *Chapter 2, Developing a Basic Site with Node.js and Express*. The difference is that this time we will use templates at the client-side part of the application. For example:

```
<script type="text/x-handlebars" data-template-name="say-hello">
  <div class="content">{{name}}</div>
</script>
```

This a template definition that Handlebar uses. It's defined in a `<script>` tag because the content inside is ignored by the browser, and it is not rendered as a part of the DOM tree. There is one expression: `{{name}}`. Normally, the template is populated with information and such parts of the markup are replaced with the actual data. What a handlebar does is that it gets the value of the `script` tag. Then, it will parse it. The expressions found are executed and the result is returned to the developer.

Understanding Ember.js

Before we continue with the actual coding of our small application, we will go through the most important components of Ember.js.

Exploring classes and objects in Ember.js

Like every framework, Ember.js has predefined objects and classes, which are at our disposal. In most cases, we will extend them and write only the custom logic, which is a part of your application. All the ready-to-use classes are under the `Ember` namespace. This means that whenever we want to use some part of the framework, we need to go through the `Ember.` notation. For example, in the class extending shown in the following code:

```
App.Person = Ember.Object.extend({
  firstname: '',
  lastname: '',
  hi: function() {
    var name = this.get("firstname") + " " + this.get("lastname");
    alert("Hello, my name is " + name);
  }
});
var person = App.Person.create();
person.set("firstname", "John");
person.set("lastname", "Black");
person.hi();
```

We defined a class called `Person`. It has two properties and only one function, which shows a message on the screen. Just after that, we created an instance of that class and called the method. The properties of a class in Ember.js are accessed via `.get` and `.set` methods. In the previous example, we were still able to use `this.firstname` instead of `this.get("firstname")`, but this is not exactly right. In the `.set` and `.get` methods, Ember.js does some calculations, which are necessary to implement features such as data binding and computed properties. If we access the variable directly, the library may not have the chance to do its job.

Computed properties

By definition, the **computed properties** are properties, which derive their value by executing a function. Let's continue and use the previous example. Instead of concatenating both `firstname` and `lastname` every time, we will create a computed property `name`, which will return the needed string. We can see this in the following code:

```
App.Person = Ember.Object.extend({
  firstname: '',
  lastname: '',
  hi: function() {
    alert("Hello, my name is " + this.get("name"));
  },
    name: function() {
        return this.get("firstname") + " " + this.get("lastname");
    }.property("firstname", "lastname")
});
var person = App.Person.create();
person.set("firstname", "John");
person.set("lastname", "Black");
person.hi();
```

We will still access a property with the `.get` method, but this time its value is calculated by a function. This can be extremely helpful if we need to format our data before displaying it. It's good to know that we can use computed properties to set a value. By default, they are read only, but we can transform them to accept and process data, as follows:

```
name: function(key, value) {
  if (arguments.length > 1) {
        var nameParts = value.split(/\s+/);
        this.set('firstname', nameParts[0]);
        this.set('lastname',  nameParts[1]);
    }
    return this.get("firstname") + " " + this.get("lastname");
}.property("firstname", "lastname")
```

Router

The routing processes are more like extensions for the other client-side frameworks. However, in Ember.js, everything is built around them. The **Router** is a class, which translates the page's URL to a series of nested templates. Each of these templates is connected to a model that delivers the data.

```
App = Ember.Application.create();
App.Router.map(function() {
  this.resource('post', { path: '/post/:post_id' }, function() {
    this.route('edit', { path: '/edit' });
    this.resource('comments', function() {
```

```
        this.route('new');
      });
    });
  });
```

The routes are grouped into resources. Let's say that we have a blog application. The previous example defines a route to every post, which has an option to edit and comment. We can nest resources if necessary. Every route has a `path` parameter, which can be skipped if it matches the name of the route. In the previous snippet, we can skip the options for the `edit` route. That's because the name of the path is the same as the route name.

We can think about the Router as a starting point of our logic. Every route and resource has its own class and controller linked to it. The good news is that we don't really need to define them because the framework does this for us. Very often, we will need to modify their implementation by setting some properties; however, in general, we are free to leave the default suggested versions. Once we start working with Ember.js, we will find out that there are a lot of classes that are automatically created. Sometimes, it is a bit difficult to follow them. There is a Google Chrome extension called **Ember Inspector**. It's actually a new tab in the Developer Tools panel. The inspector can show us what is going on in our application. For example, the previous code produces the following result:

View Tree	Route Name	Route	Controller	Template	URL
/# Routes	**application**	ApplicationRoute	ApplicationController	application	
Data	**post**	PostRoute	PostController	post	
	post.edit	PostEditRoute	PostEditController	post/edit	/post/:post_id/edit
	comments	CommentsRoute	CommentsController	comments	
	comments.new	CommentsNewRoute	CommentsNewController	comments/new	/post/:post_id/comments/new
	comments.index	CommentsIndexRoute	CommentsIndexController	comments/index	/post/:post_id/comments
	post.index	PostIndexRoute	PostIndexController	post/index	/post/:post_id
	index	IndexRoute	IndexController	index	/

As we can see, there are several routes and controllers available. There is a default route for the application and for the main **post** resource. The extension is really helpful because it shows us the exact names of the classes. Ember.js has strict naming conventions, and we should be able to figure out the names by ourselves, but it is still a handy extension.

If we want to put some logic in the controller of the comments section, then we should use the following code:

```
App.CommentsController = Ember.ObjectController.extend({
  // ...
});
```

We should remember that we are actually modifying the definition of the class. The instances of it are automatically created by the framework.

Views and templates

We already mentioned that Ember.js uses Handlebars for its templating purposes. A simple definition of a template looks like the following code:

```
<script type="text/x-handlebars" data-template-name="post/index">
  <section>
    <h1>{{title}}</h1>
    <p>{{text}}</p>
  </section>
</script>
```

It's a script tag along with the HTML markup. Every template has a `view` class associated with itself. Usually, the developers don't extend the `view` class. It is used in cases where we need to heavily handle user events or create custom components. Under the hood, the `view` class translates the primitive browser events into events that mean something in the context of our application. For example, we may have the following template:

```
<script type="text/x-handlebars" data-template-name="say-hello">
  Hello, <b>{{view.name}}</b>
</script>
```

Its corresponding View instance is seen as follows:

```
var view = Ember.View.create({
  templateName: "say-hello",
  name: "user",
  click: function(evt) {
    alert("Clicked.");
  }
});
view.append();
```

We are handling the clicking of the text. By using the `.append` method, the view is added to the `<body>` element, but there is `.appendTo`, which can add our custom HTML to whichever DOM element we need.

Models

Every route in Ember.js has an associated model, which is an object that stores the persistent state. We set our models in the route's class. There is a hook called `model`, which should return our data. Very often, we will get the application's data asynchronously. For such cases, we can return a JavaScript promise.

```
App.PostRoute = Ember.Route.extend({
  model: function() {
    return Ember.$.getJSON("/posts.json");
  }
});
```

The template linked to a specific route renders its HTML based on the model. So, we are able to use expressions that represent properties from the result of that `.model` method. For example, see the following code:

```
<script type="text/x-handlebars" data-template-name="post/index">
  <section>
    <h1>{{title}}</h1>
    <p>{{text}}</p>
  </section>
</script>

App.PostIndexRoute = Ember.Route.extend({
  model: function() {
    return {
      title: "Title of the post",
      text: "Text of the post"
    }
  }
})
```

Controllers

In the context of Ember.js, the **controllers** are classes that decorate your models with the display logic. Ideally, they will store the data that doesn't need to be stored in a database. It's only needed when the information needs to be displayed. As with the models, the framework defines a different controller class for every route. Let's say that we are developing an online book store. We could have a route like the one in the following code:

```
App.Router.map(function() {
  this.route("books");
});
```

We have only one route, but three controllers are defined. We are able to see them by using the Google Chrome's extension. Check out the following screenshot:

View Tree	Route Name	Route	Controller	Template	URL
/# Routes	**application**	ApplicationRoute	ApplicationController	application	
Data	**books**	BooksRoute	BooksController	books	/books
	index	IndexRoute	IndexController	index	/

In the `BooksRoute` class, we will define our model, and in `BooksController`, we will create computed properties to display the books in a better way. The controllers are also the place where we could process any events that come from the browser. Initially, such events are caught by the views, but if there is no defined `View` or there is no handler for the event, then that is passed to the controller.

These are the most important components of every Ember.js application. Now, let's continue to build our small project—a single-page app for getting messages from Twitter.

Writing Ember.js

The client side of the project contains two screens. The first one displays an input field and a button where the user should type the Twitter handle. The second one shows the tweets. We can see this in the following screenshot:

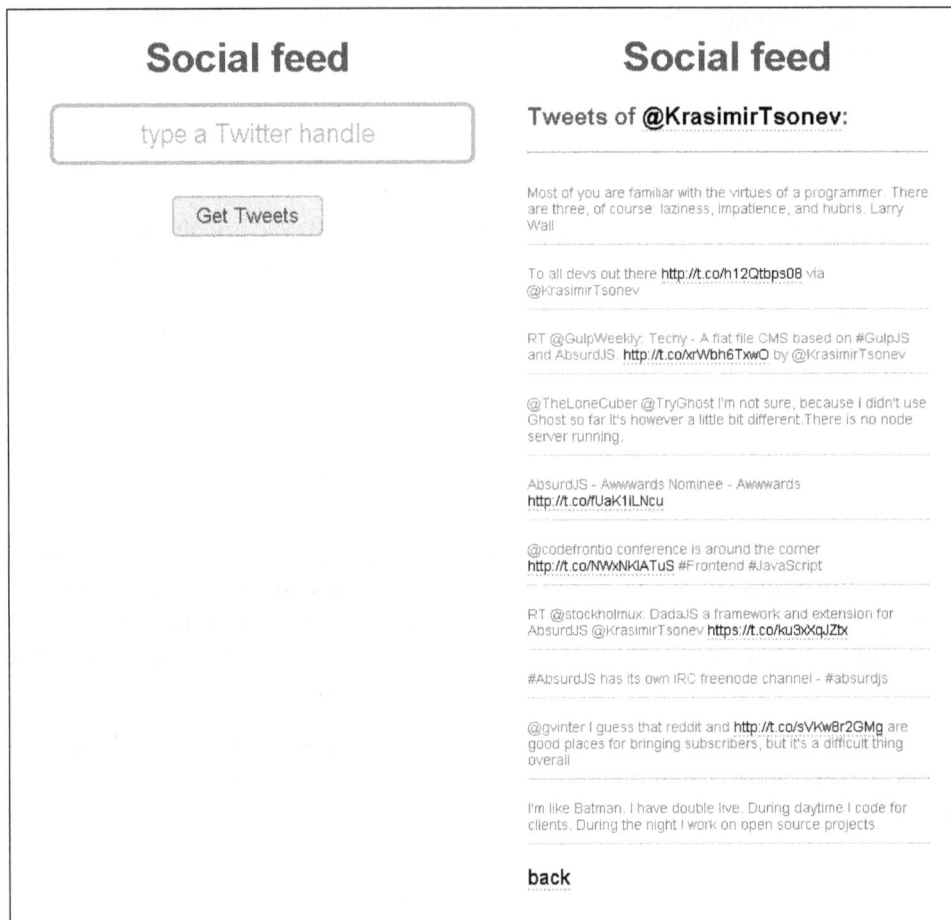

The left part of the image shows the first page and the right one shows the tweets of the user.

Defining the templates

The html/page.html file is our main file and is the base of our application and will be the first page that the user sees. It contains the following code:

```
<!doctype html>
<html>
```

```
<head>
    <title>Get Twitter Feed</title>
    <link rel="stylesheet" type="text/css" href="css/styles.css">
</head>
<body>

    <script src="js/jquery-1.10.2.js"></script>
    <script src="js/handlebars-1.1.2.js"></script>
    <script src="js/ember-1.3.1.js"></script>
    <script src="js/scripts.js"></script>
</body>
</html>
```

That's the basic HTML markup that we are starting from. The dependencies of
Ember.js are included along with the `js/scripts.js` file, which will contain our
custom logic. The templates, which we will define afterwards, will be placed inside
the `<body>` tag. The following template is the first one. It's the main template of the
application:

```
<script type="text/x-handlebars" data-template-name="social-feed">
    <div class="wrapper">
        <h1>Social feed</h1>
        <section>
            {{outlet}}
        </section>
    </div>
</script>
```

We have only one expression: `{{outlet}}`. That's an Ember.js-specific expression
and shows the framework where we want our subviews to be rendered. Note
the name of the template: `social-feed`. We will use the same name during the
definition of the routes.

The HTML code that we will use for the first screen, the one with the input field,
looks as follows:

```
<script type="text/x-handlebars" data-template-name="social-feed/
index">
    {{input
        type="text"
        value=handle
        placeholder="type a Twitter handle"
    }}
    <a href="javascript:void(0);" class="get-tweets-button" {{action
getTweets}}>Get Tweets</a>
</script>
```

The name of the template is `social-feed/index`. With `/index`, we are saying that this is the default template of the route with the name `social-feed`. The `{{input}}` tag is an Ember.js helper, which is later transformed to an `<input>` element. The `type` and `placeholder` attributes have the same meaning as in the regular HTML. However, `value` here plays another role. Note that `value` is not wrapped in double quotes. That's because the `handle` keyword is actually a property of the Route's controller, and we have two-way data binding. There is another expression used: `{{action}}`, which accepts the name of a method, which is again part of the controller. It will respond to a user's click event.

The latest template that we will define is the one that shows the tweets. We can see that template as follows:

```
<script type="text/x-handlebars" data-template-name="social-feed/
tweets">
    <h3>Tweets of {{{formattedHandle}}}:</h3>
    <hr />
    <ul>
    {{#each}}
        <li>{{formatTweet text}}</li>
    {{/each}}
    </ul>
    {{#link-to 'social-feed.index'}}back{{/link-to}}
</script>
```

The `{{{formattedHandle}}}` helper will be replaced with a link to the user's profile on Twitter. There are three brackets because the value of `formatedHandle` will be in HTML. If we use only double brackets, handlebars will display the data as string and not as HTML markup. There is an `{{#each}}` helper used. That's how we will loop through the fetched tweets and display their content. And at the end, we will use the `{{#link-to}}` helper to generate a link to the first screen.

Defining the routes

Normally, the Ember.js applications start with creating a global namespace followed by defining the routes. `js/scripts.js` starts with the following code:

```
App = Ember.Application.create();
App.Router.map(function() {
  this.resource('social-feed', { path: '/' }, function() {
    this.route("tweets", { path: '/tweets/:handle' });
  });
});
```

There is one resource and one route created. The route responds on a URL that contains a dynamic segment. Let's check the names of the controllers and templates in Ember.js Chrome extension. The following screenshot displays the exact created classes:

View Tree	Route Name	Route	Controller	Template	URL
/# Routes	application	ApplicationRoute	ApplicationController	application	
Data	loading	LoadingRoute	LoadingController	loading	/loading
	error	ErrorRoute	ErrorController	error	/_unused_dummy
	social-feed	SocialFeedRoute	SocialFeedController	social-feed	
	social-feed.loading	SocialFeedLoadingRoute	SocialFeedLoadingController	social-feed/loading	/loading
	social-feed.error	SocialFeedErrorRoute	SocialFeedErrorController	social-feed/error	/_unused_dummy
	social-feed.tweets	SocialFeedTweetsRoute	SocialFeedTweetsController	social-feed/tweets	/tweets/:handler
	social-feed.index	SocialFeedIndexRoute	SocialFeedIndexController	social-feed/index	/

Ember.js defines several routes by default: `application`, `loading`, and `error`. The first one is the main project route. `LoadingRoute` and `ErrorRoute` can be used if we have asynchronous transition between two routes. These substates are very useful if we load the model data from an external resource and want to indicate the process somehow.

Handling the user input and moving to the second screen

We need to define a controller for the `social-feed/index` template. It will transfer the user to the second screen if the button on the screen is clicked. Along with that, we will get the Twitter handle that is entered in the input element. We define a controller as follows:

```
App.SocialFeedIndexController = Ember.Controller.extend({
  handle: '',
  actions: {
    getTweets: function() {
      if(this.get('handle') !== '') {
        window.location.href = "#/tweets/" + this.get('handle');
        this.set('handle', '');
      } else {
        alert("Please type a Twitter handle.");
      }
    }
  }
});
```

Note that we are clearing the value of the `handle` property—`this.set('handle', '')`. We are doing this because the user will later return to that view and will want to enter a new username. As an addition, we can extend the view that is responsible for that template, and we can bring the browser's focus to the field once the template is added to the DOM tree.

```
App.SocialFeedIndexView = Ember.View.extend({
  didInsertElement: function() {
    this.$('input').focus();
  }
});
```

Displaying the tweets

We have a URL address that responds with a JSON-formatted list of tweets. There are corresponding controllers and route classes, which are defined by default from Ember.js. However, we need to set a model and get the handle from the browser's address, so we will create our own classes. This can be seen as follows:

```
App.SocialFeedTweetsRoute = Ember.Route.extend({
  model: function(params) {
    this.set('handle', params.handle);
    return Ember.$.getJSON('/tweets/' + params.handle);
  },
  setupController: function(controller, model) {
    controller.set("model", model);
        controller.set("handle", this.get('handle'));
  }
});

App.SocialFeedTweetsController = Ember.ArrayController.extend({
  handle: '',
  formattedHandle: function() {
    return "<a href='http://twitter.com/" + this.handle + "'>@" +
this.handle + '</a>';
  }.property('handle')
});
```

The dynamic segment from the URL comes to the Route's `model` function in the `params` argument. We will get the string and set it as a property of the class. Later, when we set up the controller, we are able to pass it along with the model. The `setupController` function is a hook, which is run during the route's initialization. As we said in the beginning of the chapter, the main role of the controller is to decorate the model. Ours does only one thing—it defines a computed property that prints the Twitter handle of the user in a `<a>` tag. The controller also extends `Ember.ArrayController`, which provides a way to publish a collection of objects.

If we go back a few pages and check out the `social-feed/tweets` template, we will see that we can show the tweets with the following code:

```
{{#each}}
  <li>{{formatTweet text}}</li>
{{/each}}
```

Normally, we will use only `{{text}}` and not `{{formatTweet text}}`. What we did is used a custom-defined helper, which will format the text of the tweet. We need that because the tweet can contain URLs, and we want to transform them to valid HTML links. We can do that as part of the controller and define another computed property, but we will do it as a Handlebars helper. We can see it as follows:

```
Ember.Handlebars.registerBoundHelper('formatTweet', function(value) {
  var exp = /(\b(https?|ftp|file):\/\/[-A-Z0-9+&@#\/%?=~_|!:,.;]*[-
A-Z0-9+&@#\/%=~_|])/ig;
    return new Handlebars.SafeString(value.replace(exp, "<a
href='$1'>$1</a>"));
});
```

We are using a regular expression to transform the URLs to the `<a>` tags.

With the latest lines of the code, our `js/script.js` file is finished, and we can use the application to fetch the latest tweets of any Twitter user.

Summary

In this chapter, we learned how to use Node.js with Ember.js. We successfully created a fully working application, which shows the messages posted on Twitter. Essential work was done by external modules, which again proves that the Node.js ecosystem is really flexible and provides everything we need to develop top-notch web applications. The modern client-side frameworks such as Ember.js, AngularJS, or Backbone.js are expected to receive JSON and Node.js is capable of delivering it.

In the next chapter, we will find out how to use Node.js to optimize our project tasks and boost our coding performance.

8
Developing Web App Workflow with Grunt and Gulp

In the last few chapters, we learned how to use Node.js together with the most popular client-side JavaScript frameworks such as AngularJS and Ember.js. We learned how to run a fully functional web server and build a command-line tool.

In this chapter, we will explore the world of the task runners. Grunt and Gulp are two modules widely used and they have a solid collection of plugins.

Introducing the task runners

Applications are agreeably complex in nature. More and more logic is put into the browser and it is written with many lines of JavaScript code. The new CSS3 features and the improved performance of native browser animations lead to a lot of CSS code. Of course, at the end, we still want to keep the things separated. Make sure that everything is well-placed in different folders and files. Otherwise, our code will be difficult to maintain. We may need to generate `manifest.json`, use a preprocessor, or simply copy files from one location to another. Thankfully, there are instruments that make our life easier. The **task runner** accepts instructions and performs certain actions. It enables us to set a watcher and monitor files for changes. This is extremely helpful if we have a complex setup and a lot of aspects to handle.

At the moment, there are two popular task runners for Node.js: Grunt and Gulp. They are widely used because of the plugins written specifically for them; the modules themselves don't have many features; however, if we combine them with external plugins, they become our best friends. Even companies such as Twitter or Adobe elaborate on them.

Exploring Grunt

Grunt is a Node.js module, which means it is installed via the Node.js package manager. To get started, we need to install Grunt's command-line tool.

```
npm install -g grunt-cli
```

The -g flag sets the module as a global command so that we can run it in every directory. Once the installation finishes, we are able to run grunt, which is executable. The instructions to the task runner are stored in the Gruntfile.js file. Place this file in the root project's directory and place our tasks inside. Once we have filled the Grunt file, open the terminal, navigate to the directory, and type grunt.

The Grunt's configuration file is like a rules list. Describe step by step what exactly needs to be done. The following code snippet is the simplest format of the Gruntfile.js file:

```
module.exports = function(grunt) {
  grunt.initConfig({
    concat:{
    }
  });
  grunt.registerTask('default', ['concat']);
}
```

The tasks are set up in the object passed to the initConfig function. In the preceding example, we have only one task, concat. The same task is added to the default set of rules. These rules will be run when we start Grunt.

As mentioned, these task runners are so powerful because of the huge collection of plugins made by the developers. To add a plugin to our Grunt setup, include it in our package.json file. This is because the plugin is again a Node.js module. In the next section of this chapter, we will use the grunt-contrib-concat plugin and merge several JavaScript files into one. The following code snippet is how the package.json file should look like:

```
{
  "name": "GruntjsTest",
  "version": "0.0.1",
  "description": "GruntjsTest",
  "dependencies": {},
  "devDependencies": {
    "grunt-contrib-concat": "0.3.0"
  }
}
```

After running `npm install`, we will be able to request the plugin by calling `grunt.loadNpmTasks (grunt-contrib-concat)`. There is also a `grunt.loadTasks` method for custom-defined tasks. Now, let's continue and run our first Grunt script.

Concatenating files

Concatenation is one of the most common operations. It is the same with the CSS styles. Having many files means more server requests, which could decrease the performance of your application. The `grunt-contrib-concat` plugin is here to help. It accepts a `glob` pattern of source files and a destination path. It goes through all the folders, finds the files that match the pattern, and merges them. Let's prepare a folder for our small experiment.

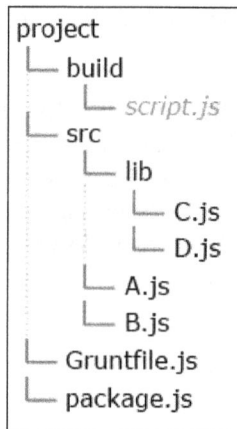

```
project
    └── build
            └── script.js
    └── src
            └── lib
                    └── C.js
                    └── D.js
            └── A.js
            └── B.js
    └── Gruntfile.js
    └── package.js
```

The `build/scripts.js` file will be generated by Grunt. So, we don't have to create it. Add some content to the files in the `src` folder. Our `Gruntfile.js` file should contain the following code:

```javascript
module.exports = function(grunt) {
  grunt.initConfig({
    concat: {
      javascript: {
        src: 'src/**/*.js',
        dest: 'build/scripts.js'
      }
    }
  });
  grunt.loadNpmTasks('grunt-contrib-concat');
  grunt.registerTask('default', ['concat']);
}
```

The `concat` task contains a `javascript` object that holds the configuration for the concatenation. The source value is actually a `glob` pattern that matches all the JavaScript files inside the `src` folder and its subfolders. We have used the `glob` module in *Chapter 6, Using Node.js as a Command-line Tool*. With the preceding code, we can run the `grunt` command in our terminal. We will get a result similar to what is shown in the following screenshot:

```
$ grunt
Running "concat:javascript" (concat) task
File "build/scripts.js" created.

Done, without errors.
```

The `scripts.js` file should be generated in the `build` directory and contain all the files from the `src` folder.

Very often, we end up debugging the compiled file. This is mainly because it's the file that we use in the browser and everything is saved together, so we can't really see where the error is initiated. In such cases, it is good to add some text before the content in every file. This will allow us to see the original destination of the code. The new content of the `Gruntfile.js` file is as follows:

```
module.exports = function(grunt) {
  grunt.initConfig({
    concat: {
      javascript: {
        options: {
          process: function(src, filepath) {
            return '// Source: ' + filepath + '\n' + src;
          }
        },
        src: 'src/**/*.js',
        dest: 'build/scripts.js'
      }
    }
  });
  grunt.loadNpmTasks('grunt-contrib-concat');
  grunt.registerTask('default', ['concat']);
}
```

Thus, we pass a custom `process` function. It accepts the content of the file and its path. It should return the code we want to be concatenated. In our case, we just add a short comment at the top.

Minifying your code

Minification is a process that makes our code smaller. It uses smart algorithms that replace the names of our variables and functions. It also removes the unnecessary spaces and tabs. That's pretty important for optimization because it normally decreases the file size by half. Grunt's plugin, `grunt-contrib-uglify`, provides this functionality. Let's use the example code from the previous pages and modify our `Gruntfile.js` file as follows:

```javascript
module.exports = function(grunt) {
  grunt.initConfig({
    concat: {
      javascript: {
        options: {
          process: function(src, filepath) {
            return '// Source: ' + filepath + '\n' + src;
          }
        },
        src: 'src/**/*.js',
        dest: 'build/scripts.js'
      }
    },
    uglify: {
      javascript: {
        files: {
          'build/scripts.min.js': '<%= concat.javascript.dest %>'
        }
      }
    }
  });
  grunt.loadNpmTasks('grunt-contrib-concat');
  grunt.loadNpmTasks('grunt-contrib-uglify');
  grunt.registerTask('default', ['concat', 'uglify']);
}
```

In the preceding code, we do the following important tasks:

- We add `grunt-contrib-uglify` to our `package.json` file
- We run `npm install` to get the module in the `node_modules` directory
- At the end, we define the minification's options

In the preceding code, we set up a new task called `uglify`. Its property, `files`, contains a hash of the conversions we want to perform. The key is the destination path and the value is the source file. In our case, the source file is the output of another task so that we can directly use the `<% %>` delimiters. We are able to set the exact path, but doing it using the delimiters is much more flexible. This is because we may end up with a very long Grunt file and it is always good to keep the code maintainable. If we have the destination in one place only, we are able to correct it without repeating the same change in other places.

Note that the tasks we defined depend on each other, that is, they should be run in a specific order. Otherwise, we will receive unexpected results. Like in our example, the `concat` task is performed before `uglify`. That's because the second one needs the result from the first.

Watching files for changes

Grunt is really great at doing some stuff for us. However, it is a bit annoying if we have to run it every time we change some of our files. Let's take the situation in the previous section. We have a bunch of JavaScript scripts and want to merge them into one file. If we work with the compiled version, then we have to run the concatenation every time we make corrections to the source files. For such cases, the best thing to do is set up a watcher—a task that monitors our filesystems and triggers a specific task. A plugin called `grunt-contrib-watch` does exactly this for us. Add this to our `package.json` file and run `npm install` again to install it locally. Our file needs only one entry in the configuration. The following code shows the new watch property:

```
module.exports = function(grunt) {
  grunt.initConfig({
    concat: {
      javascript: {
        options: {
          process: function(src, filepath) {
            return '// Source: ' + filepath + '\n' + src;
          }
        },
        src: 'src/**/*.js',
        dest: 'build/scripts.js'
      }
    },
    uglify: {
      javascript: {
        files: {
          'build/scripts.min.js': '<%= concat.javascript.dest %>'
```

```
          }
        }
      },
      watch: {
        javascript: {
          files: ['<%= concat.javascript.src %>'],
          tasks: ['concat:javascript', 'uglify']
        }
      }
    });
    grunt.loadNpmTasks('grunt-contrib-concat');
    grunt.loadNpmTasks('grunt-contrib-uglify');
    grunt.loadNpmTasks('grunt-contrib-watch');
    grunt.registerTask('default', ['concat', 'uglify', 'watch']);
}
```

There is a watch task added after concat and uglify. Note that the plugin requires two options. The first one, files, contains the files we want to monitor and the second one, tasks, defines the processes that will be run. We are also executing a specific part of the concat task. At the moment, we have only one thing to concatenate, but if we work on a big project, we may have several types of files or even different JavaScript sources. So, it is always good to specify our definitions, especially for the watching glob patterns. We really don't want to run unnecessary tasks. For example, we normally don't concatenate JavaScript if some of the CSS files are changed.

If we use the setup shown in the preceding code and run Grunt, we will see the output as shown in the following screenshot:

There is pretty good logging that shows what exactly happened. All the tasks are run and the src\A.js file is changed. Immediately, the concat and uglify plugins are launched.

Ignoring files

Sometimes, we will have files that should not occupy a part in the whole process, for example, having a CSS file should not be concatenated with the others. Grunt offers a solution for such cases. Let's say we want to skip the JavaScript in src/lib/D.js. We should update our GruntFile.js file and change the src property of the task:

```
concat: {
  javascript: {
    options: {
      process: function(src, filepath) {
        return '// Source: ' + filepath + '\n' + src;
      }
    },
    src: ['src/**/*.js', '!src/lib/D.js'],
    dest: 'build/scripts.js'
  }
}
```

All we have to do is to use an array instead of a single string. The exclamation mark in front of the value tells Grunt that we want this file to be ignored.

Creating our own task

Grunt has an enormous collection of plugins and we will probably find what we want. However, there are situations where we need something custom for our projects. In such cases, we will need a custom task. Let's say we need to save the file size of the compiled JavaScript. We should access build/scripts.js, check its size, and write it to a file on the hard disk.

The first thing we need is a new directory that will host our tasks as shown in the following screenshots:

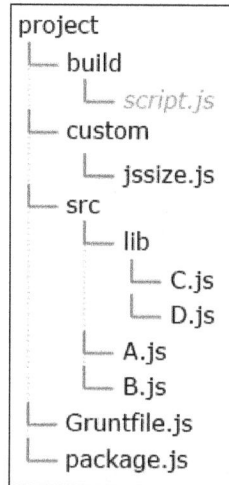

```
project
 └── build
       └── script.js
 └── custom
        └── jssize.js
 └── src
      └── lib
            └── C.js
            └── D.js
         └── A.js
         └── B.js
   └── Gruntfile.js
   └── package.js
```

Note the `custom` folder and the `jssize.js` file. Its name may not match that of the new task, but it is a good practice to keep them in sync. Before writing the actual code that does the job, we will change our configuration to fire the task. So far, we used `grunt.loadNpmTasks` to indicate modules we will use during the processing. However, our script is not part of the Node.js' package management and we have to use `grunt.loadTasks`. The method accepts a path to the folder containing our file as shown in the following lines of code:

```
grunt.loadNpmTasks('grunt-contrib-concat');
grunt.loadNpmTasks('grunt-contrib-uglify');
grunt.loadNpmTasks('grunt-contrib-watch');
grunt.loadTasks('custom');
```

All the files in the `custom` directory will be fetched and registered as valid, ready-to-use plugins. Now we can add our `jssize` task to the default tasks list so that it runs along with the others as follows:

```
grunt.registerTask('default', ['concat', 'uglify', 'jssize',
'watch']);
```

At the end, we will add a new entry in the object passed to the `grunt.initConfig` function as follows:

```
jssize: {
  javascript: {
    check: 'build/scripts.js',
    dest: 'build/size.log'
  }
}
```

As this is our own task, we can pass whatever we think is necessary. In our case, this is the file we will get the size of and the path we will save the result in.

A Grunt task is actually a Node.js module that exports a function by accepting the Grunt's API object. The following is the content of the `custom/jssize.js` file:

```
var fs = require('fs');
module.exports = function(grunt) {
    grunt.registerMultiTask('jssize',
      'Checks the JavaScript file size', function() {
        var fileToCheck = this.data.check;
        var destination = this.data.dest;
        var stat = fs.statSync(fileToCheck);
        var result = 'Filesize of ' + fileToCheck + ': ';
        result += stat.size + 'bytes';
        grunt.file.write(destination, result);
    });
};
```

The key moment is the `grunt.registerMultiTask` method. The first argument is the name of the task. This is quite important because the same string is used in the `Gruntfile.js` file. Immediately after, we pass a description and anonymous function. The body of that function contains the real logic to accomplish the task. The configurations we defined are available in the `this.data` object. The file-size check is done and the result is saved via the `grunt.file` API.

Generating a cache manifest file

We found out how to create our own Grunt task. Let's write something interesting. Let's generate a cache manifest file for the project.

The Cache manifest file is a declarative file we use to indicate the static resources of our web application. This could be our CSS files, images, HTML templates, video files, or something that remains consistent. This is a huge optimization trick because the browser will load these resources not from the web, but from the user's device. If we need to update an already cached file, we should change the manifest.

At the moment, we have only JavaScript files. Let's add a few images and one CSS file. Make the necessary changes so that our project folder looks like the following figure:

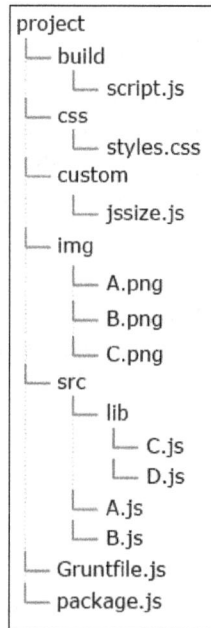

```
project
└── build
        └── script.js
└── css
        └── styles.css
└── custom
        └── jssize.js
└── img
        └── A.png
        └── B.png
        └── C.png
└── src
        └── lib
            └── C.js
            └── D.js
        └── A.js
        └── B.js
└── Gruntfile.js
└── package.js
```

The content of `styles.css` is not important. The images in the `img` folder are also not important. We just need different files to test with. The next thing we have to do is add our task to `Gruntfile.js`. We will use `generate-manifest` as a name as shown in the following code snippet:

```
'generate-manifest': {
  manifest: {
    dest: 'cache.manifest',
    files: [
      'build/*.js',
      'css/styles.css',
      'img/*.*'
    ]
  }
}
```

Of course, we should not forget to add the task to the `default` list as shown in the following code snippet:

```
grunt.registerTask('default', ['concat', 'uglify',
    'jssize', 'generate-manifest', 'watch']);
```

Note that we are passing several `glob` patterns; these are the files we want to add. Describing every single file in the configuration will take too much time and we could forget something. Grunt has a really effective API method, `grunt.file.expand`, that accepts `glob` patterns and returns the matched files. The rest of our task is to compose the content of the manifest file and save it to the disc. We will register the new task and fill the `content` variable, which is later written to the file, as follows:

```
module.exports = function(grunt) {
    grunt.registerMultiTask('generate-manifest',
        'Generate manifest file', function() {

        var content = '',
            self = this,
            d = new Date();

        content += 'CACHE MANIFEST\n';
        content += '# created on: ' + d.toString() + '\n';
        content += '# id: '
            + Math.floor((Math.random()*1000000000)+1) + '\n';

        var files = grunt.file.expand(this.data.files);
        for(var i=0; i<files.length; i++) {
            content += '/' + files[i] + '\n';
        }
        grunt.file.write(this.data.dest, content, {});

    });
};
```

It's a good practice to rely on the Grunt API in our custom tasks. It keeps the consistency of our application because we depend only on one module—Grunt. In the preceding code, we used `grunt.file.expand`, which we already discussed before the code, and `grunt.file.write` that saves the manifest's content to the disk.

To provide a workable manifest, the cache file should start with CACHE MANIFEST. That's why we add it at the beginning. It's also a good practice to include the date on which the generation happened. The randomly generated id simplifies the process of an application's development.

As mentioned, the browser will serve the cached version of the files until the cache manifest file is changed. Setting a different id each time forces the browser to fetch the latest version of the files. However, in the production environment, this should be removed. To use the cache manifest file, add a special attribute in our HTML page as follows:

```
<html manifest="cache.appcache">
```

If everything goes well, we should see a result similar to that shown in the following screenshot:

```
Running "concat:javascript" (concat) task
File "build/scripts.js" created.

Running "uglify:javascript" (uglify) task
File build/scripts.min.js created.

Running "jssize:javascript" (jssize) task

Running "generate-manifest:manifest" (generate-manifest) task

Running "watch" task
Waiting...
```

Hence, the content of the cache manifest will be as follows:

```
CACHE MANIFEST
# created on: Fri Feb 14 2014 23:40:46 GMT+0200
  (FLE Standard Time)
# id: 585038007
/build/scripts.js
/build/scripts.min.js
/css/styles.css
/img/A.png
/img/B.png
/img/C.png
```

Documenting our code

We know that the code should have documentation. But very often, this is too time consuming and mundane. There are some good practices out there that we could use. One of them is to write comments into the code and generate the documentation using these comments. Following this approach, we should make our code more understandable for our colleagues. The Grunt plugin, `grunt-contrib-yuidoc`, will help us create the .doc files. Add it to our `package.json` and run `npm install`. Again, all we have to do is to update our `Gruntfile.js` file.

```
yuidoc: {
  compile: {
    name: 'Project',
    description: 'Description',
    options: {
      paths: 'src/',
      outdir: 'docs/'
    }
  }
}
...
grunt.registerTask('default', ['concat', 'uglify',
  'jssize', 'generate-manifest', 'yuidoc', 'watch']);
```

There is a `paths` property that shows the source code and the `outdir` property that shows where the documentation will be saved. If we run Grunt and navigate to the directory with our favorite browser, we will see that there is nothing listed. That's because we didn't add any comment to the code. Open `src/A.js` and place the following code:

```
/**
 * This is the description for my class.
 *
 * @class A
 */
var A = {
  /**
   * My method description.
     Like other pieces of your comment blocks,
   * this can span multiple lines.
   *
   * @method method
   */
  method: function() {

  }
};
```

After relaunching the tasks, we will see the **A Class** in the documentation as shown in the following screenshot:

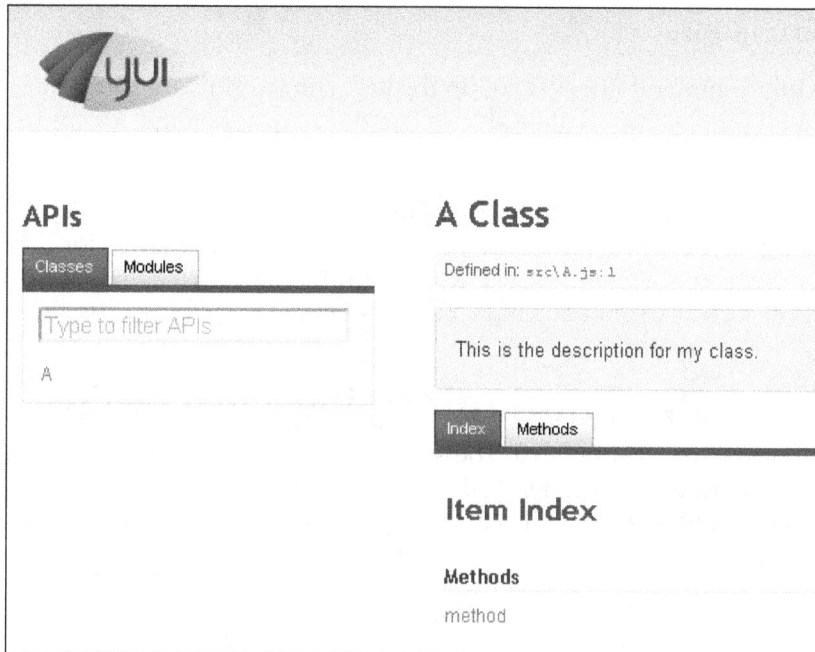

Discovering Gulp

Gulp is a build system that has become quite popular. It's almost the same concept as Grunt. We are able to create tasks that do something for us. Of course, there are a lot of plugins. In fact, most of the main Grunt plugins have equivalent plugins in Gulp. However, there are some differences, which are mentioned in the following points:

- There is a configuration file, but it is called `gulpfile.js`

- Gulp uses streams to process the files, which means that it doesn't create any temporary file or folder. This may lead to the better performance of the task runner.

- Gulp follows the `code-over-configuration` principle, that is, while we set up the Gulp tasks, the process is like coding rather than writing the configurations. This makes Gulp friendly for the developers.

Installing Gulp and fetching plugins

Like Grunt, Gulp is available in the Node.js' package manager.

```
npm install -g gulp
```

The preceding command line will set up the task runner globally. Once the installation is complete, we will be able to run the `gulp` command. Of course, we should do that in the directory containing the `gulpfile.js` file.

The plugins for Gulp are also Node.js modules. For example, `gulp-concat` is the same as `grunt-contrib-concat` and `gulp-uglify` is the alternative for `grunt-contrib-uglify`. It is a good practice to describe them in a `package.json` file. There is no function such as `grunt.loadNpmTasks`. We could directly require the module.

Concatenating and minifying with Gulp

Let's use the code we already have. There are a bunch of JavaScript files in the `src` folder and we want them concatenated. The task runner should also generate a minified version and watch the files for changes. We will need several modules, and here is how our `package.json` file looks like:

```
{
    "name": "GulpTest",
    "version": "0.0.1",
    "description": "GulpTest",
    "dependencies": {},
    "devDependencies": {
        "gulp": "3.5.2",
        "gulp-concat": "2.1.7",
        "gulp-uglify": "0.2.0",
        "gulp-rename": "1.0.0"
    }
}
```

The `gulp` command is needed because we need access to Gulp's API. The `gulp-concat` plugin will concatenate the files and `gulp-uglify` will minify the result. The `gulp-rename` plugin is used because we have to deliver two files—one suitable for reading and one minified, that is, `build/scripts.js` and `build/scripts.min.js`.

The following code is the content of the `gulpfile.js` file:

```
var gulp = require('gulp');
var concat = require('gulp-concat');
var uglify = require('gulp-uglify');
var rename = require('gulp-rename');
```

```
gulp.task('js', function() {
  gulp.src('./src/**/*.js')
  .pipe(concat('scripts.js'))
  .pipe(gulp.dest('./build/'))
  .pipe(rename({suffix: '.min'}))
  .pipe(uglify())
  .pipe(gulp.dest('./build/'))
});

gulp.task('watchers', function() {
  gulp.watch('src/**/*.js', ['js']);
});

gulp.task('default', ['js', 'watchers']);
```

With Grunt, we need a little more knowledge about the task runner and its configuration structure. With Gulp, it's slightly different. We have the usual Node.js modules and the usage of their public APIs. The script starts with the definition of the plugins and the `gulp` object. A task is defined by using the `gulp.task` method. The first parameter is the name of the task and the second is a function. Also, instead of the function, we may pass an array of strings representing other tasks.

Similarly, like in Grunt, we have a `default` entry. This time, we split the tasks into two parts: JavaScript operations and watchers. Almost every Gulp task starts with `gulp.src` and ends with `gulp.dest`. The first method accepts the `glob` pattern, showing the files that need to be transformed. The `gulp.dest` plugin saves the result to the desired location. All the actions between them are actually modules that receive and output the streams. In our case, the `js` task fetches all the files from the `src` directory and its subfolders, concatenates them, and saves the result to the `build` folder. We continue by renaming the file, minifying it, and saving it in the same place. The output of our terminal after running `gulp` in the project's folder should be as shown in the following screenshot:

Of course, we should see the `scripts.js` and `scripts.min.js` files in the build directory.

Creating your own Gulp plugin

The development of the Gulp plugin looks almost the same as creating a Grunt one. We need a new Node.js module with a proper API. The difference is that we receive a stream and we should then output the stream. This can be a little difficult to code because we need to understand how the streams work. Thankfully, there is a helper package that simplifies the process. We are going to use `through2` — a tiny wrapper around the Node.js' streams API. So, our `package.json` file grows a bit with the following content:

```
{
  "name": "GulpTest",
  "version": "0.0.1",
  "description": "GulpTest",
  "dependencies": {},
  "devDependencies": {
    "gulp": "3.5.2",
    "gulp-concat": "2.1.7",
    "gulp-uglify": "0.2.0",
    "gulp-rename": "1.0.0",
    "through2": "0.4.1"
  }
}
```

Let's create the same `jssize` task. It needs to do only one job: measure the file size of the concatenated file. We could recreate the `custom` directory and place an empty `jssize.js` file there. Our Gulp file also needs a quick correction. At the top, we require the newly created module as follows:

```
var jssize = require('./custom/jssize');
```

We have to pipe the output of the first `gulp.dest('./build/')` command to the `jssize` plugin. The following snippet shows the finished task:

```
gulp.task('js', function() {
  gulp.src('./src/**/*.js')
  .pipe(concat('scripts.js'))
  .pipe(gulp.dest('./build/'))
  .pipe(jssize())
  .pipe(rename({suffix: '.min'}))
  .pipe(uglify())
  .pipe(gulp.dest('./build/'));
});
```

Now, let's see how our plugin looks using the following code:

```
var through2 = require('through2');
var path = require('path');
var fs = require("fs");
module.exports = function () {
    function transform (file, enc, next) {
        var stat = fs.statSync(file.path);
        var result = 'Filesize of ' + path.basename
            (file.path) + ': ';
        result += stat.size + 'bytes';
        fs.writeFileSync
            (__dirname + '/../build/size.log', result);
        this.push(file);
        next();
    }
    return through2.obj(transform);
};
```

The `through2.obj` object returns a stream used in the Gulp's pipeline. Working with streams is like working with chunks. In other words, we do not receive the entire file, but parts of it again and again till we get the whole data. The `through2` object simplifies the process and gives us direct access to the entire file. So, the `transform` method accepts the file, its encoding, and a function that we need to call once we finish our job. Otherwise, the chain will be stopped and the next plugins will not be able to finish their tasks. The actual code that generates the `size.log` file is the same as that used in the Grunt version.

Summary

In this chapter, we learned how to use the task runners. These are tools that make our life easier by simplifying the common tasks. As web developers, we might want to concatenate and minify our production code, and such trivial operations are well-handled by modules such as Grunt and Gulp. The wide range of plugins and the great Node.js community encourage the usage of task runners and change our workflow completely.

In the next chapter, we will dive into test-driven development and see how Node.js handles such processes.

9
Automate Your Testing with Node.js

In the previous chapter, we learned how to work with Grunt and Gulp to automate our development process. These two Node.js modules have a huge collection of plugins, which we can use in almost every case. In this chapter, we will talk about testing, its importance, and how to integrate it in our workflow. The following is a list of topics that we will cover:

- Popular testing methodologies
- The Jasmine framework
- The Mocha framework
- Testing with PhantomJS and DalekJS

Understanding the importance of writing tests

When developing software, the code we write can be put in the browser, run as a desktop program, or started as a Node.js script. In all these cases, we expect specific results. Every line of code has some significance, and we need to know whether the final product will do the job. Normally, we debug our applications, that is, we write part of the program and run it. By monitoring the output or its behavior, we assess whether everything is okay or whether there is a problem. However, this approach is time-consuming, especially if the project is big. Iterations through every single feature of the application costs a lot of time and money. Automated testing helps in such cases. From an architectural viewpoint, testing is very important. That's because when the system is complex and we have numerous relationships between the modules, it is difficult to add new features or introduce major changes.

We can't really guarantee that everything will work as it worked before the modifications. So, instead of relying on manual testing, it is much better to create scripts that can do this for us. Writing tests has several major benefits, as follows:

- This proves that our software is stable and works as expected.
- This saves a lot of time because we don't have to repeatedly perform manual testing.
- A badly written code with a lot of dependencies cannot be tested easily. Writing tests in most of these cases leads to better code.
- If we have a solid test suite, we can extend the system without worrying about damaging something.
- If the tests cover all the application's features, then they can be used as the application's documentation.

Choosing a testing methodology

There are few popular ways of writing tests. Let's see which are they and the differences between them.

Test-driven development

Test-driven development (TDD) is a process that relies on the repetition of short development cycles. In other words, we write our test while writing the implementation. The shorter the cycles, the better. The following diagram shows the TDD flow:

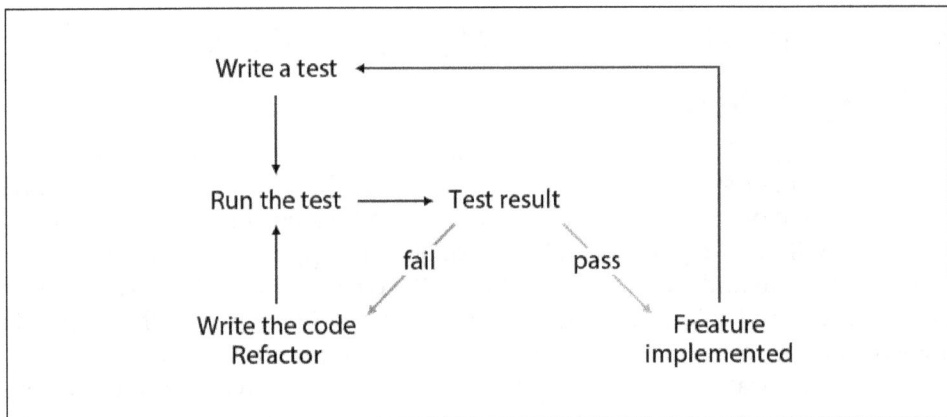

Before we write the actual code that does the job for us, we need to prepare a test. Of course, after the first run, the test will fail because nothing has been implemented. So, we need to ensure that the test passes all the cycles. Once this happens, we may spend some time refactoring what has been done so far and continue with the next method, class, or feature. Note that everything spins around the test, which is a really good thing because this is where we define what our code should do. With this as a basis, we avoid delivering unnecessary code. We can also be sure that the implementation meets the requirements.

Behavior-driven development

Behavior-driven development (BDD) is similar to TDD. In fact, if the project is a small one, we can't really spot the differences. The idea of this approach is to focus more on the specification and the application's processes, rather than the actual code. For example, if we test a module that posts messages on Twitter with TDD, we will probably ask the following questions:

- Is the message empty?
- Is the message length less than 140 symbols?
- Is the Ajax request made properly?
- Does the returned JSON contain certain fields?

However with BDD, we ask only the following question:

- Is the message sent to Twitter?

Both processes are interrelated and, as we said, sometimes there is no difference at all. What we should remember is that BDD focuses on what the code is doing and TDD on how the code is doing it.

Classifying tests

There are several types of tests that you may write, which evaluate our system by giving an input and expecting a specific output. However, they also perform this evaluation on different parts. It is good to know their names, which are listed as follows:

- **Unit testing**: Unit testing performs checks on a single part of the application; it focuses on one unit. Often, we face difficulties in writing such tests because we can't split our code into units; this is usually a bad sign. If there is no clearly defined module, we can't proceed with such tests. Distributing the logic to different units not only helps in testing but also contributes to the overall stability of the program. Let's illustrate the problem with the following diagram:

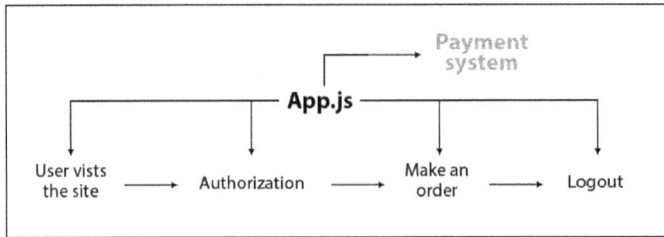

Let's assume we have an e-commerce site that sells products to our users. In the preceding diagram, processes such as log in, ordering, and logout are handled by one class, defined in the App.js file. Yes, it works. We may achieve the goal and successfully close the circle, but this is absolutely not unit testable because there are no units. It is much better if we split the responsibilities into different classes, as shown in the following diagram:

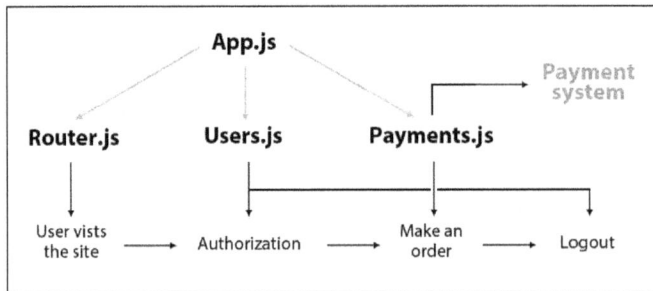

We continue to use App.js and it still controls everything. However, the different parts of the whole flow are divided between three classes: Router, Users, and Payments. Now, we are able to write unit tests.

- **Integration testing**: Integration tests output a result for several units or components. If we look at the preceding example, the integration test will simulate the whole process of ordering a product, that is, logging in, buying, and logging out. Normally, integration tests use several modules of the system and ensure that the modules work properly together.

- **Functional testing**: The functional tests are closely related to integration tests and focus on a specific functionality in the system. It may involve several modules or components.

- **System testing**: The system tests test our program in different environments. In the context of Node.js, this could be when running our scripts on different operating systems and monitoring the output. Sometimes there are differences and if we want to globally distribute our work, we need to ensure that our program is compatible with the most popular systems.

- **Stress or performance testing**: These tests evaluate our application beyond the defined specifications and show how our code reacts to heavy traffic or complex queries. They are really helpful when making a decision about the program's architecture or choosing a framework.

There are some other types of testing, but the previously mentioned testing methods are the most popular. There is no strict policy on what tests to write. Of course, there are good practices, but what we should focus on is writing a testable code. There is nothing better than an application fully covered with tests.

As testing is a really important part of the development process, there are frameworks specifically oriented toward writing tests. In general, when we use a framework, we need the following two tools:

- **Test runner**: This is the part of the framework that runs our tests and displays messages whether they pass or fail.

- **Assertions**: These methods are used for the actual checks, that is, if we need to see whether an variable is `true`, then we can write `expect(active)`. `toBe(true)` instead of just `if(active === true)`. It's better for the reader and also prevents some strange situations; for example, if we want to see whether a variable is defined or not, the `if` statement in the following code returns `true` because the `status` variable has a value and this value is `null`. In fact, we are asking whether the `status` variable initialized, and if we leave the test in this manner, we will get wrong results. That's why we need an assertion library that has proper methods for testing. The following code is the example that shows that the `status` variable is actually defined and its type is `object`:

```
var status = null;
if(typeof status != "undefined") {
```

```
        console.log("status is defined");
    } else {
        console.log("status is not defined");
    }
```

Using Jasmine

Jasmine is a framework to test the JavaScript code. It is available as a Node.js module and also as a library, which we can use in the browser. It comes with its own assertion methods.

Installing Jasmine

We are going to use the Node.js version of the framework. It's a module, so it can be installed via the Node.js package manager, npm, as shown in the following code line:

```
npm install jasmine-node -g
```

The preceding command will set up Jasmine globally, so we can run `jasmine-node` in every directory of our choice. The tests could be organized into different files placed in one folder or in subfolders. The only requirement is to end the filenames with `spec.js`, for example, `testing-payments.spec.js` or `testing-authorization.spec.js`.

Defining the module for testing

Before we write the actual test, let's define the application we want to build. Let's say we need a Node.js module that reads a file and finds specific words inside it. The following is the basic file structure that we are starting from:

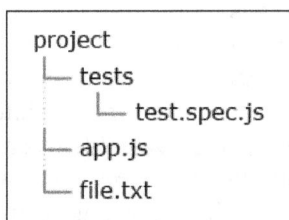

```
project
 └─ tests
        └─ test.spec.js
 └─ app.js
 └─ file.txt
```

The code that tests the application will be placed in `tests/test.spec.js`, the implementation of the logic will be in `app.js`, and the file that we will read from will be `file.txt`. Let's open the `file.txt` file and add the following text inside:

```
The quick brown fox jumps over the lazy dog.
```

That's a phrase used to test typewriter's keys. It contains all the letters from the English alphabet and is perfect for our small project.

Following the test-driven development concept

The task is simple and we can probably solve it in around 20 lines of code. For sure, we can wrap all the code in one function and perform everything there. The downside is that if something goes wrong, we can't detect where the problem occurs. That's why we will split the logic into two parts and test them separately in the following ways:

- Reading the file's content
- Searching for a certain word inside the file's content

As we explained in the beginning of this chapter, we will write the test first, we will see it fail, and then will write the code for app.js.

Testing the file-reading process

Writing tests, just like any other task, can be challenging. Sometimes, we can't determine what to test and what to exclude. There is a certain unsaid rule that advices users to avoid working on features that are tested by other developers—in our example, we need not test whether the file is read successfully. If we do that, it will look like we are testing the filesystem API of Node.js, which is not necessary.

Every test written with Jasmine starts with the `describe` clause. Add the following code to `tests/test.spec.js`:

```
describe("Testing the reading of the file's content.", function() {
  // ...
});
```

The `describe` method accepts a description and a function. In the body of this function, we will add our assertions. Keep in mind that the text that we add needs to be informative because it will be displayed if the test fails. Similar to the `describe` block, we have to add the `it` blocks. These blocks contain the actual commands for testing, as shown in the following code snippet:

```
describe("Testing the reading of the file's content.", function() {
  it("should create an instance of app.js", function(done) {
    var app = require("../app.js");
```

```
        expect(app).toBeDefined();
        done();
    });
});
```

We are adding meaningful information that tells what exactly we are going to test. The second argument of `it` is again a function. The difference is that it accepts an argument, which is another function. We need to call it once we are done with the checks. Many scripts in JavaScript are asynchronous, and the `done` callback helps us in handling such operations.

The preceding code block includes the `app.js` module and verifies the result. The `expect` method accepts a subject of the assertion, and the following chained methods perform the actual check.

We have a test ready, so we can execute it. Run `jasmine-node ./tests` and you will see the following result:

```
Finished in 0.02 seconds
1 test, 1 assertion, 0 failures, 0 skipped
```

The test case passes. The `app.js` file is empty, but even then Node.js doesn't fail. The value of the `app` variable is actually an empty object. Let's continue and try to imagine the methods that we will need. In the following code we are adding one more block testing a `read` API method of the module:

```
describe("Testing the reading of the file's content.", function() {
    it("should create an instance of app.js", function(done) {
        var app = require("../app.js");
        expect(app).toBeDefined();
        done();
    });
    it("should read the file", function(done) {
        var app = require("../app.js");
        var content = app.read("./file.txt");
        expect(content).toBe("The quick brown fox jumps over the lazy
            dog.");
        done();
    });
});
```

The first it runs well but the second one raises an error. That's because there is nothing in app.js. We don't have a read method there. The error is shown in the following screenshot:

```
Failures:

  1) Testing the reading of the file's content. should read the file
    Message:
      TypeError: Object #<Object> has no method 'read'
    Stacktrace:
      TypeError: Object #<Object> has no method 'read'
```

Note that we can clearly see what went wrong. If someone, for some reason, deletes or renames the used method, this test will fail. Even if the function exists, we expect to see a specific result that validates the job of the module.

Now, we have to start writing the actual code of the application. We should make the test passing. Place the following code in app.js:

```
module.exports = {
   read: function(filePath) {

   }
}
```

If we run the test, it will fail but for another reason, and that's because there is no logic inside the read method. The following screenshot is the result in the console:

```
Failures:

  1) Testing the reading of the file's content. should read the file
    Message:
      Expected undefined to be 'The quick brown fox jumps over the lazy dog.'.
    Stacktrace:
      Error: Expected undefined to be 'The quick brown fox jumps over the lazy do
g.'.
```

This time the read method is defined, but it doesn't return anything and expect(content).toBe("The quick brown fox jumps over the lazy dog.") fails. Let's read file.txt with the Node.js file API and return its content:

```
var fs = require('fs');
module.exports = {
   read: function(filePath) {
     return fs.readFileSync(filePath).toString();
   }
}
```

Now, the color of the test is in green, which indicates that the module has the method we used and that method returns what we expect, as shown in the following screenshot:

```
Finished in 0.007 seconds
2 tests, 2 assertions, 0 failures, 0 skipped
```

Finding strings in the file content

By using the same methodology, we will implement the second part of our application: finding words inside the file. The following is the new `describe` block, which we will start with the following code:

```
describe("Testing if the file contains certain words", function() {
    it("should contains 'brown'", function(done) {
        var app = require("../app.js");
        var found = app.check("brown", "The quick brown fox jumps over
            the lazy dog.");
        expect(found).toBe(true);
        done();
    });
});
```

We require a `check` method that accepts two arguments. The first one is the word we want to find, and the second one is the string that will contain it. Note that we are not using the `read` method. The idea is to test the function separately and guarantee that it works properly. This is a very important step because it makes our `check` method universal. It is not bound to the idea of matching the text inside a file; however, it does match the text inside a string. If we don't use the test-driven workflow, we may end up with one function that does both the operations: reading the file and scanning its content. However, in our case, we can use the same module with the text fetched from a database or via an HTTP request. And, if we find that our module doesn't find a particular word, we will know that the problem lies in the `check` function because it is tested as separate unit.

The following is the code of the new method:

```
var fs = require('fs');
module.exports = {
    read: function(filePath) {
        return fs.readFileSync(filePath).toString();
    },
    check: function(word, content) {
```

```
        return content.indexOf(word) >= 0 ? true : false;
    }
}
```

The test is now passed with three assertions as shown in the following screenshot:

```
Finished in 0.02 seconds
3 tests, 3 assertions, 0 failures, 0 skipped
```

Writing an integration test

The tests we have written so far were unit tests, that is, they tested the two units of our application. Now, let's add an integration test. Again, we need a failing test that uses the module. So, we are starting with the following code:

```
describe("Testing the whole module", function() {
    it("read the file and search for 'lazy'", function(done) {
        var app = require("../app.js");
        app.read("./file.txt")
        expect(app.check("lazy")).toBe(true);
        done();
    });
});
```

Note that we are not keeping the content of the file in a temporary variable, and we are not passing it to the check method. In fact, we are not interested in the actual content of the file. We are interested only if it contains a specific string. So, our module should handle this and keep the text in it. The preceding test fails and the following message is displayed:

```
Failures:

  1) Testing the whole module read the file and search for 'lazy'
   Message:
     TypeError: Cannot call method 'indexOf' of undefined
   Stacktrace:
     TypeError: Cannot call method 'indexOf' of undefined
```

The following are the changes needed to make app.js work as we want it to:

```
var fs = require('fs');
module.exports = {
    fileContent: '',
    read: function(filePath) {
```

```
    var content = fs.readFileSync(filePath).toString();
    this.fileContent = content;
    return content;
  },
  check: function(word, content) {
    content = content || this.fileContent;
    return content.indexOf(word) >= 0 ? true : false;
  }
}
}
```

We will simply store the text in a local variable named `fileContent`. Note that we are making changes carefully and keeping the return logic of the `read` method. This is needed because there is a test that requires this functionality. This shows one more benefit of TDD. We ensure that the code, before including our modifications, works in its original form. In complex systems or applications, this is extremely important, and without tests, this will be really difficult to achieve. The final result is again a screenshot with a green message:

```
Finished in 0.01 seconds
4 tests, 4 assertions, 0 failures, 0 skipped
```

Testing with Mocha

Mocha is a little more advanced testing framework than Jasmine. It is more configurable, supports TDD or BDD testing, and even has several types of reporters. It is also quite popular and portable for client-side usage in the browser, which makes it a good candidate for our testing.

Installation

Similar to Jasmine, we need the Node.js's package manager to install Mocha. By running the following command, the framework will be set up globally:

```
npm install -g mocha
```

Once the installation finishes, we can run `mocha ./tests`. By default, the tool searches for JavaScript files and tries to run them. Here, let's use the same example used with Jasmine and pass it through Mocha. It actually uses the same syntax of the `describe` and `it` blocks. However, it doesn't come with its own assertion library. In fact, there is a built-in Node.js module for such purposes named `assert`. There are also libraries developed by other developers, for example, `should.js`, `chai`, or `expect.js`.

They differ in certain aspects but do the same job: checking actual and expected values and raising an error if they don't match. After that, the framework catches the error and displays the results.

Translating our example using Mocha

If we run the same tests with `mocha ./tests`, we will get the following result:

```
0 passing (7ms)
4 failing

  1) Testing the reading of the file's content. should create an instance of app
.js:
     ReferenceError: expect is not defined
```

The tests fail because there is no assertion library, that is, the `expect` function is not available. Let's use the default `assert` module of Node.js as shown in the following code snippet:

```javascript
var assert = require("assert");
describe("Testing the reading of the file's content.", function() {
  it("should create an instance of app.js", function(done) {
    var app = require("../app.js");
    if(typeof app == "undefined") {
      assert.fail('undefined', 'object');
    }
    done();
  });
  it("should read the file", function(done) {
    var app = require("../app.js");
    var content = app.read("./file.txt");
    assert.equal(content, "The quick brown fox jumps over the lazy
      dog.");
    done();
  });
});
```

Everything is the same but the `expect` module calls are replaced with `assert.equal`. We used `assert.fail` to notify the framework that there is something wrong. The following are the other `describe` blocks:

```javascript
describe("Testing if the file contains certain words", function() {
  it("should contains 'brown'", function(done) {
    var app = require("../app.js");
```

```
    var found = app.check("brown", "The quick brown fox jumps over
        the lazy dog.");
    assert.equal(found, true);
    done();
    });
});
describe("Testing the whole module", function() {
    it("read the file and search for 'lazy'", function(done) {
        var app = require("../app.js");
        app.read("./file.txt")
        assert.equal(app.check("lazy"), true);
        done();
    });
});
```

With the latest changes, the tests should pass and we should see the
following screenshot:

```
4 passing (8ms)
```

Selecting a reporter

Mocha is quite flexible when we talk about reporters. The reporter is the part of the
framework that displays the results on the screen. There are a dozen of options we
can choose from. To set the type of the reporter, we should use the -R option in the
command line, for example, the closest thing to Jasmine's reporter is the dot type, as
shown in the following screenshot:

```
$ mocha .\tests -R dot

    . . . .

4 passing (7ms)
```

To see more detailed information about the passed or failed tests, we can use the
spec reporter as shown in the following screenshot:

```
Testing the reading of the file's content.
  √ should create an instance of app.js
  √ should read the file

Testing if the file contains certain words
  √ should contains 'brown'

Testing the whole module
  √ read the file and search for 'lazy'


4 passing (10ms)
```

There is also a reporter that looks like a landing plane (the `landing` type) as shown in the following screenshot:

```
-------------------------------------------------------------------
.................................................................⊀
-------------------------------------------------------------------

4 passing (10ms)
```

Testing with a headless browser

So far we learned how to test our code. We can write a module, class, or library, and if it has an API, we can test it. However, if we need to test a user interface, it gets a little bit complex. Frameworks such as Jasmine and Mocha can run the code we write but can't visit a page, click a button, or send a form; at least, not alone. For such testing, we need to use a headless browser. A headless browser is a web browser without a user interface. There is a way to control it programmatically and perform actions such as accessing DOM elements, clicking on links, and filling forms. We are able to do the same things as we use a real browser. This gives us a really nice instrument to test the user interface. In the next few pages, we will see how to use a headless browser.

Writing the subject of our test

In order to explore the possibilities of such testing, we need a simple site. Let's create two pages. The first one will contain an input field and a button. The second page will be visited when the button on the first one is clicked. The page's h1 tag title will change depending on the text written in the field. Create a new directory and insert the following code in the app.js file:

```
var http = require('http');
var url = require('url');
```

```
var port = 3000;
var pageA = '\
  <h1>First page</h1>\
  <form>\
    <input type="text" name="title" />\
    <input type="submit" />\
  </form>\
';
var pageB = '\
  <h1>{title}</h1>\
  <a href="/">back</a>\
';
http.createServer(function (req, res) {
  var urlParts = url.parse(req.url, true);
  var query = urlParts.query;
  res.writeHead(200, {'Content-Type': 'text/html'});
  if(query.title) {
    res.end(pageB.replace('{title}', query.title));
  } else {
    res.end(pageA);
  }
}).listen(port, '127.0.0.1');
console.log('Server running at http://127.0.0.1:' + port);
```

We need only two of the Node.js native modules to launch our server. The `http` module runs the server, and the `url` module gets the GET parameters from the URL. The markup of the pages is stored in simple variables. There is a check in the handler of the HTTP request, which serves `pageB` if the form on `pageA` is submitted. If we run the server with `node app.js`, we will see how the pages look, as shown in the following screenshot:

Note that the text entered in the text field is set as the title of the second page. There is also a **back** button we can use to return to the home page. We have a subject to run our tests on. We'll define the actions we need to verify as follows:

- Is the page properly rendered? We should check whether the tags of `pageA` are actually on the page.

- We should add some string to the text field and submit the form.

- The title of the newly loaded page should match the text that we entered.

- We should be able to click on the **back** button and return to the home page.

Testing with PhantomJS

We know how our application is suppose to work, so let's write the tests. The headless browser we will use is **PhantomJS**. Visit `http://phantomjs.org` and download the package suitable for your operating system. Like we did for Node.js, we will write our test in a JavaScript file and run it at the command line. Let's say that our file structure looks like the following diagram:

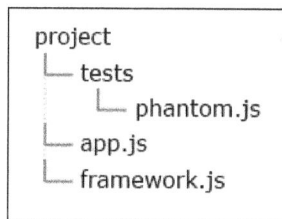

```
project
 └─ tests
       └─ phantom.js
 └─ app.js
 └─ framework.js
```

Keep in mind that PhantomJS is not a Node.js module. The JavaScript code we write for PhantomJS is not exactly a valid Node.js code. We can't directly use native modules such as `assert`. Also, there isn't a test runner or test framework integrated. It's a browser based on **Webkit** but controlled from the command line or via the code. It comes across as binary, and once it is installed, we will be able to run the `phantom ./tests/phantom.js` command in our terminal. The test code will open `http://127.0.0.1:3000` and will interact with the pages there. Of course, the JavaScript community developed tools to combine testing frameworks such as Jasmine or Mocha with PhantomJS, but we are not going to use them in this chapter. We will write our own small utility — that's what the `framework.js` file is for.

Developing the micro testing framework

The final result should be a simple function ready to use, such as `describe` or `it`, in Jasmine. It should also have something similar to the assertion library so we don't have to use the usual `if-else` statements or report the failing test manually. In the following code, we can see the proper implementation:

```
var test = function(description, callback) {
  console.log(description);
  callback(function(subject) {
    return {
      toBe: function(value) {
```

```
        if(subject !== value) {
          console.log("! Expect '" + subject + "' to be '" + value
            + "'.")
        }
      },
    toBeDefined: function() {
      if(typeof subject === 'undefined') {
        console.log("! Expect '" + subject + "' to be defined")
        }
      }
    }
  });
}
```

The function accepts description and function. The first argument is just printed out to the console, which indicates what we are going to test. Just after that, we call the passed `callback` function with another function as the parameter, which plays the role of an assertion library. It accepts the subject of testing and executes two methods against it: `toBe` and `toBeDefined`. The following is a simple usage:

```
test("make a simple test", function(expect) {
  var variable = { property: 'value' };
  expect(true).toBe(true);
  expect(1).toBe(0);
  expect(variable.property).toBeDefined()
  expect(variable.missing).toBeDefined()
});
```

If we run the preceding code, the result will be as shown in the following screenshot:

```
make a simple test
! Expect '1' to be '0'.
! Expect 'undefined' to be defined
```

Understanding how PhantomJS works

PhantomJS accepts instructions written in JavaScript. We can save them to a file and execute them via the command line by using the `phantom` command. Let's look at the following code snippet:

```
var page = require('webpage').create();
var url = 'http://127.0.0.1:3000';
page.onConsoleMessage = function(msg) {
  // ...
};
```

```
page.onLoadFinished = function(status) {
  // ...
};
page.open(url);
```

The `page` variable is an access to the PhantomJS API. There is a method, `open`, which loads a new page. We are mostly interested in two events dispatched from the headless browser. The first one, `onConsoleMessage`, is fired when the loaded page uses the `console` command, for example, `console.log` or `console.error`. The second event, `onLoadFinished`, is also quite important. We have a function that is called when the page is loaded. That's the place where we should place our tests. Along with listening for events, we are going to use the following two other methods of PhantomJS:

- `injectJs`: This method requires path to a file on our hard disk. The passed file is included on the page. We may also use `includeJs` that does the same thing, but it loads the file from an external source.

- `Evaluate`: This method accepts a function that is executed in the context of the currently loaded page. This is important because we need to check whether certain elements are in the DOM tree. We need to interact with them by filling in the text field and clicking on a button.

Writing the actual test

Before we start using PhantomJS, we need to run our application with `node ./app.js`. By doing this, we are running a server that listens on a particular port. PhantomJS will make requests to that server. Now, let's start filling in the `tests/phantom.js` file as follows:

```
var page = require('webpage').create();
var url = 'http://127.0.0.1:3000';
page.onConsoleMessage = function(msg) {
  console.log("\t" + msg);
};
page.onLoadFinished = function(status) {
  console.log("phantom: load finished");
  page.injectJs('./framework.js');
    phantom.exit();
};
page.open(url);
```

As we have already discussed, we are able to create a `page` variable and open a particular URL. In our case, we are using the address of the test application. The `onConsoleMessage` listener just prints out the message to our terminal. When the page loads, we inject our micro unit testing framework. This means that we are able to call the `test` function in the context of the page. If we run the script with `phantom ./tests/phantom.js`, we will get the following result:

```
$ phantomjs .\tests\phantom.js
phantom: load finished
```

The preceding screenshot shows exactly what should happen. The browser goes to the page and fires `onLoadFinished`. It's important to call `phantom.exit();` otherwise, PhantomJS's process will stay active.

The `framework.js` file is injected to the page and we can write the first test, that is, to check whether the title contains **First page**, fill in the test field, and submit the form:

```
page.onLoadFinished = function(status) {
  console.log("phantom: load finished");
  page.injectJs('./framework.js');
  page.evaluate(function() {
    test("should open the first page", function(expect) {
      expect(document).toBeDefined();
      expect(document.querySelector('h1').innerHTML).toBe('First
        page');
      document.querySelector('input[type="text"]').value =
        'Phantom test';
      document.querySelector('form').submit();
    });
  });
  phantom.exit();
};
```

The function that is executed by the `evaluate` method is run in the context of the page, so it gets an access to the usual document object. We are able to use the `getElementById`, `querySelector`, or `submit` methods. The script's result obtained now is as shown in the following screenshot:

```
$ phantomjs .\tests\phantom.js
phantom: load finished
         should open the first page
```

Now it gets interesting. Indeed, the form is submitted, but we immediately called `phantom.exit()`, which terminates our script. If we remove it, the browser will stay active and the `onLoadFinished` event will be fired again because a new page is successfully loaded. However, the script fails because there is no text field or a `form` element on the next page. We need to evaluate another function. The following is one of the possible solutions:

```
var steps = [
  function() {
    test("should open the first page", function(expect) {
      expect(document).toBeDefined();
      expect(document.querySelector('h1').innerHTML).toBe('First
        page');
      document.querySelector('input[type="text"]').value =
        'Phantom test';
      document.querySelector('form').submit();
    });
  },
  function() {
    test("should land on the second page", function(expect) {
      expect(document).toBeDefined();
      expect(document.querySelector('h1').innerHTML).toBe('Phantom
        test');
      var link = document.querySelector('a');
      var event = document.createEvent('MouseEvents');
      event.initMouseEvent('click', true, true, window, 1, 0,
        0);
      link.dispatchEvent(event);
    });
  },
  function() {
    test("should return to the home page", function(expect) {
      expect(document.querySelector('h1').innerHTML).toBe('First
        page');
    });
  }
];
page.onLoadFinished = function(status) {
  console.log("phantom: load finished");
  page.injectJs('./framework.js');
  page.evaluate(steps.shift());
  if(steps.length == 0) {
    console.log("phantom: browser terminated");
    phantom.exit();
  }
};
```

The `steps` array is a global variable that contains a series of functions that need to be evaluated. On every `onLoadFinished` event, we are fetching one of those functions until the `steps` array is empty. This is where we call `phantom.exit()` as shown in the following screenshot:

```
$ phantomjs .\tests\phantom.js
phantom: load finished
        should open the first page
phantom: load finished
        should land on the second page
phantom: load finished
        should return to the home page
phantom: browser terminated
```

PhantomJS opens the home page. It enters **Phantom test** in the text field and submits the form. Then, on the next page, it checks whether the title contains the valid value, and when you click on the **back link** button, it loads the previous page again.

Testing with DalekJS

So far we learned how to test our JavaScript code. After that, we found out how to write user interface tests with Phantom.js. All these are really helpful, but it will be even better if we are able to run a real browser and control it. With DalekJS, this is possible. It's a really nice Node.js module that comes with a command-line interface tool and submodules for major browsers such as Google Chrome, Firefox, and Internet Explorer.

Let's see how everything works and install the command-line tool of DalekJS using the following command:

```
npm install -g dalek-cli
```

After running the preceding command, we will have the `dalek` command set up in our terminal. Let's copy the files used in the PhantomJS test and replace `framework.js` with a `package.json` file. We will also rename `tests/phantom.js` to `tests/dalek.js`. So, the following is the new file structure:

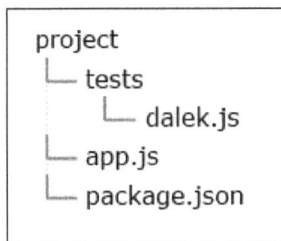

```
project
└── tests
    └── dalek.js
└── app.js
└── package.json
```

The application we will use will be the same. DalekJS supports several browsers, including Google Chrome, so we will use it. Of course, we should have it installed on our system. The following code snippet shows how the `package.json` file looks:

```json
{
    "name": "project",
    "description": "description",
    "version": "0.0.1",
    "devDependencies": {
        "dalekjs": "*",
        "dalek-browser-chrome": "*"
    }
}
```

A quick `npm install` command will create the `node_modules` directory with both dependencies included in it. DalekJS has a detailed documentation published on `http://dalekjs.com`. It states that we can load pages, fill forms, and click on different DOM elements. It also comes with its own testing API, so we don't have to think about this. The test we have to write is actually pretty short. The following is the content of `tests/dalek.js`:

```js
var url = 'http://127.0.0.1:3000';
var title = 'DalekJS test';
module.exports = {
    'should interact with the application': function (test) {
        test
        .open(url)
        .assert.text('h1', 'First page', 'The title is "First page"')
        .type('input[type="text"]', title)
        .submit('form')
        .assert.text('h1', title, 'The title is "' + title + '"')
        .click('a')
        .assert.text('h1', 'First page', 'We are again on the home
          page')
        .done()
    }
};
```

Again, we will make a request to `http://127.0.0.1:3000` and expect to see certain elements on the page. We will also enter some text inside the text field (the `type` method) and submit the form (the `submit` method). To run the test, we need to type in the following command:

```
dalek .\tests\dalek.js -b chrome
```

If we skip the -b parameter, DalekJS will use Phantom.js. That's the default browser type of the library. When the preceding command is launched at the terminal, a new instance of the Google Chrome browser is opened. It executes what we defined in the test and closes the browser. In order to get the example working, we need to run the application by executing node ./app.js. The result is reported to the console as shown in the following screenshot:

```
Running tests
Running Browser: Google Chrome
OS: Windows NT 6.1 x86_64
Browser Version: 33.0.1750.117

RUNNING TEST - "should interact with the application"
> OPEN http://127.0.0.1:3000
* TEXT The title is "First page"
> TYPE input[type="text"]
> SUBMIT form
* TEXT The title is "DalekJS test"
> CLICK a
* TEXT We are again on the home page
* 3 Assertions run
* TEST - "should interact with the application" SUCCEEDED

 3/3 assertions passed. Elapsed Time: 1.53 sec
```

We can even make screenshots of the current browser's screenshot. It's simply calling the screenshot API method as shown in the following code snippet:

```
test
.open(url)
.assert.text('h1', 'First page', 'The title is "First page"')
.type('input[type="text"]', title)
.submit('form')
.assert.text('h1', title, 'The title is "' + title + '"')
.screenshot('./screen.jpg')
.click('a')
.assert.text('h1', 'First page', 'We are again on the home page')
.done()
```

In the preceding code, we are making a screenshot of the second page, the one that is loaded after the form is submitted.

Summary

In this chapter, we saw how important testing is. Thankfully, there are great tools available in the Node.js ecosystem. Frameworks such as Jasmine and Mocha make our life easier. Instruments such as Phantom.js save a lot of time by automating the testing and putting our code in a browser context. With DalekJS, we can even run tests directly in Firefox, Google Chrome, or Internet Explorer.

In the next chapter, we will see how to write flexible and modular CSS. Node.js has few great modules oriented for the frontend developers who write a lot of CSS.

10
Writing Flexible and Modular CSS

In the previous chapter, we learned about the most popular testing instruments under Node.js. We saw the importance of writing tests and learned about TDD and BDD. This chapter will be about **CSS (Cascading Style Sheets)** and the usage of preprocessors. The Web is built on the basis of three languages—HTML, CSS, and JavaScript. As part of modern technology, Node.js provides really helpful instruments to write CSS; in this chapter, we will have a look at these instruments and how they can improve our style sheets. This chapter will cover the following topics:

- Popular techniques to write modular CSS
- The Less preprocessor
- The Stylus preprocessor
- The Sass preprocessor
- The AbsurdJS preprocessor

Writing modular CSS

CSS has changed a lot in the last few years. Developers used CSS2 as a declarative language to decorate the page. Today's CSS3 gives us many more capabilities. Nowadays, CSS is used widely to implement design ideas animating elements on the page or even applying logic such as hiding and showing content blocks. A lot of CSS code requires better architecture, file structuring, and proper CSS selectors. Let's explore a few concepts that could help with this.

BEM (block, element, modifier)

BEM (`http://bem.info/method/definitions`) is a naming convention introduced by Yandex back in 2007. It became a popular concept to develop frontend applications. In fact, it is not only applicable for CSS but also for any other language because it has very few rules that work well.

Let's say we have the following HTML markup:

```
<header class="site-header">
    <div class="logo"></div>
    <div class="navigation"></div>
</header>
```

The instant CSS which we can come up with is as follows:

```
.site-header { ... }
.logo { ... }
.navigation { ... }
```

However, it will probably not work really well because we may have another logo in the sidebar of the page. Of course, we could use descendant selectors such as `.site-header { ... }` and `.logo { ... }`, but these come with a new problem. It is not really a good practice to connect selectors in a tree because we can't extract a part of it and use it somewhere else. BEM solves this problem by defining rules which we can follow. A block in the context of BEM is an independent entity. It can be a simple one or a compound one (containing other blocks). In the previous example, the `<header>` tag precedes the CSS block. The elements are placed inside the block and they are context-dependent, that is, they mean something only if they are placed inside the block which they belong to. The `.logo` and `.navigation` selectors in the block are the elements. There is one more type of selector called **modifiers**. To better understand them, we will use an example. Let's say that Christmas will arrive soon and we need to make a holiday version of the logo. At the same time, we need to keep the old styles because after a few months we need to revert it to its previous version. This is what modifiers are made for. We apply them on already existing elements to set a new look or style. The same can be said for a button, which has a normal, pressed, or disabled state. To separate the different types of selectors, BEM introduces the following syntax:

```
.site-header { ... } /* block */
.site-header__logo { ... } /* element */
.site-header__logo--xmas { ... } /* modifier */
.site-header__navigation { ... } /* element */
```

The name of the elements is added with double underscores and modifiers with double dashes.

Using the Object Oriented CSS approach

Object Oriented CSS (OOCSS) (`https://github.com/stubbornella/oocss/wiki`) is another concept which helps us write better CSS. It was originally introduced by Nicole Sullivan and defines the following two principles.

Separate structure and skin

Consider the following CSS:

```
.header {
    background: #BADA55;
    color: #000;
    width: 960px;
    margin: 0 auto;
}
.footer {
    background: #BADA55;
    text-align: center;
    color: #000;
    padding-top: 20px;
}
```

There are styles that describe the look and skin of the elements. The duplication is a good reason to extract them in a separate definition. Continue the preceding code as follows:

```
.colors-skin {
    background: #BADA55;
    color: #000;
}
.header {
    width: 960px;
    margin: 0 auto;
}
.footer {
    text-align: center;
    padding-top: 20px;
}
```

It's nice that we can use the same `.colors-skin` class against other elements or even better, we can change the whole theme of the page with just one little modification in that particular class.

Separate container and content

The idea is that every element should have its styles applied no matter what context it is put in. Let's use the following code as an example:

```
.header .login-form {
  margin-top: 20px;
  background: #FF0033;
}
```

At some point, we may need to put the same form in the footer of the site. The `20px` value and the `#FF0033` color, which we applied, will be lost because the form does not live in the header anymore. So, avoiding such selectors will help us to prevent such situations. Of course, we can't follow this principle for every element, but it is a really good practice overall.

Scalable and modular architecture for CSS

Jonathan Snook introduced another interesting approach called **Scalable and modular architecture for CSS (SMACSS)** (`http://smacss.com/`). His idea was to categorize the styles of the application into different categories as follows:

- **Basic selectors**: Basic selectors such as those for float clearing or the base font sizes
- **Layout**: The CSS styles defining the grid of the page
- **Modules**: These are similar to the BEM block, that is, a group of elements that form a meaningful block
- **State**: CSS styles that define the state of the elements, for example, pressed, expanded, visible, hidden, and so on
- **Theme**: Theme rules are similar to the state rules in which they describe how modules or layouts might look

Constructing the style sheet in this manner organizes the selectors very well. We can create different directories or files for the different categories, and in the end we will have everything properly set up.

Atomic design

Atomic design (`http://bradfrostweb.com/blog/post/atomic-web-design`), a concept presented by Brad Frost, is a simple but really powerful approach. We know that the basic unit of matter is an atom. Applying this to CSS, we can define the atom as a simple HTML tag:

```
<label>Search the site</label>
```

The atom contains some basic styling such as color, font size, or line height. Later, we can combine the atoms into molecules. The following example shows how a `form` tag is made of few atoms:

```
<form>
    <label>Search the site</label>
    <input type="text" placeholder="enter keyword" />
    <input type="submit" value="search" />
</form>
```

Properly styling and combining little blocks brings flexibility. If we follow this concept, we can reuse the same atoms again and again or put any molecule in a different context. Brad Frost didn't stop here. He continued by saying that the molecules can be merged into organisms and the organisms into templates. For example, the login form and the main-menu molecules define an organism header.

All the concepts mentioned in this section are not ideal for every project. However, all of them have something valuable to use. We should try not to follow them strictly but get the rules which fit best in our current application.

Exploring CSS preprocessors

Preprocessors are tools that accept code and compile it. In our context, such instruments output CSS. There are few big benefits of using preprocessors.

- **Concatenation**: Writing everything in one single `.css` file is not an option anymore. We all need to split our styles logically and this normally happens by creating a bunch of different files. CSS has a mechanism to import one file from another — the `@import` directive. However, by using it, we are forcing the browser to create another HTTP request to the server, which can decrease the performance of our application. CSS preprocessors normally deliver only one file by replacing the functionality of `@import` and simply concatenating all the used files.

- **Extending**: We don't like to write things over and over again and with pure CSS coding, this happens all the time. The good news is that preprocessors provide a feature that solves this problem. It's called a mixin. We can think of it as a function which is executed and all the styles defined in it are applied to the selector which calls it. We will see how this works in practice further in this chapter.

- **Configuration**: Normally, we need to repeat colors, widths, and font sizes all over the CSS file. By using the CSS preprocessor, we can put these values in variables and define them in only one place. Switching to a new color scheme or typography can happen really fast.

The syntax used in most preprocessors is similar to the normal CSS. This allows developers to start using them almost immediately. Let's check out the available CSS preprocessors.

Using Less

Less is a CSS preprocessor based on Node.js. It is distributed as a Node.js module and can be installed using the following command line:

```
npm install -g less
```

After the successful installation, we should be able to call the `lessc` command in the terminal. Create a new `styles.less` file somewhere and put the following code inside it:

```
body {
    width: 100%;
    height: 100%;
}
```

If we run `lessc ./styles.less`, we will see the same CSS shown as a result. The approach, which is taken by Less, is to use a syntax close to the one used in the normal CSS. So, in practice, every existing CSS code could be compiled by Less, which comes in handy, because we can start using it without doing any preparation.

Defining variables

The variables in Less are defined as we write the CSS properties. We just have to put the @ sign in front of the property's name, as shown in the following code snippet:

```
@textColor: #990;
body {
    width: 100%;
    height: 100%;
    color: @textColor;
}
```

Using mixins

Mixins are very useful when we want to transfer specific styles from one place to another or even several places. Let's say, for example, that we have constant borders that need to be set for different elements on our page. We will then use the following code snippet:

```
.my-border() {
    border-top: solid 1px #000;
```

```
    border-left: dotted 1px #999;
  }
  .login-box {
    .my-border();
  }
  .sidebar {
    .my-border();
  }
```

We can skip the brackets of `.my-border` but then we will have the same class in the resulted file. The code, as it is now, is compiled as follows:

```
.login-box {
  border-top: solid 1px #000;
  border-left: dotted 1px #999;
}
.sidebar {
  border-top: solid 1px #000;
  border-left: dotted 1px #999;
}
```

The mixins can accept parameters, which makes them one of the most important features in Less.

```
.my-border(@size: 2px) {
  border-top: solid @size #000;
  border-left: dotted @size #999;
}
.login-box {
  .my-border(4px);
}
.sidebar {
  .my-border();
}
```

In the example, the size of the border is passed as a parameter. It also has a default value of two pixels. The result after the compilation is as follows:

```
.login-box {
  border-top: solid 4px #000000;
  border-left: dotted 4px #999999;
}
.sidebar {
  border-top: solid 2px #000000;
  border-left: dotted 2px #999999;
}
```

Structuring the styles into nested definitions

Very often, when we use descendent selectors, we end up with a really long style definition. This is annoying because we have to type more and it is difficult to read. CSS preprocessors solve that problem by allowing us to write nested styles. The next code shows how we may nest selectors:

```
.content {
  margin-top: 10px;
  p {
    font-size: 24px;
    line-height: 30px;
    a {
      text-decoration: none;
    }
    small {
      color: #999;
      font-size: 20px;
    }
  }
}
.footer {
  p {
    font-size: 20px;
  }
}
```

This is much easier to understand and follow. We don't have to worry about collisions either. For example, the paragraph in the `.content` element will have a 24-pixel font size and will not be mixed with the styles of the footer. That's because at the end, we have properly generated selectors:

```
.content {
  margin-top: 10px;
}
.content p {
  font-size: 24px;
  line-height: 30px;
}
.content p a {
  text-decoration: none;
}
.content p small {
  color: #999;
  font-size: 20px;
}
```

```
.footer p {
  font-size: 20px;
}
```

Less has a dozen other features such as math calculation, function definitions, conditional mixins, and even loops. We can write a whole new book on this topic. A full list of all the functionalities can be seen at http://lesscss.org/, which is the official site of Less and contains its documentation.

Using Sass

There is another popular CSS preprocessor called **Sass**. It's actually not based on Node.js but on Ruby. So, we need to install Ruby first. You can also find detail information about how to install Ruby on the official download page: https://www.ruby-lang.org/en/downloads. Once we have it properly set up, we need to run the following command to get Sass:

```
gem install sass
```

After the execution, we have a command-line instrument installed, that is, sass, and we can run it against a .sass or .scss file. The syntax used in the .sass files looks like the one used in Stylus (we will learn about this in the *Using Stylus* section), and the syntax used in the .scss file is similar to the Less variant. At first, Less and Sass look pretty similar. Sass uses the $ sign in front of the variables, while Less uses the @ sign. Sass has the same features as Less—conditional statements, nesting, mixins, extending. The following code is a short example:

```
$brandColor: #993f99;

@mixin paragraph-border($size, $side: '-top') {
  @if $size > 2px {
    border#{$side}: dotted $size #999;
  } @else {
    border#{$side}: solid $size #999;
  }
}

body {
  font-size: 20px;
  p {
    color: $brandColor;
    @include paragraph-border(3px, '-left')
  }
}
```

The preceding code produces the following CSS code:

```css
body {
    font-size: 20px;
}
body p {
  color: #993f99;
  border-top: dotted 3px #999;
}
```

There are two keywords: `@mixin` and `@include`. The first one defines the mixin and the second one is needed during its usage.

Using Stylus

Stylus is another popular CSS preprocessor written in Node.js. Similar to Less, Stylus also accepts the usual CSS syntax. However, it introduces another type of writing — without braces, colons, and semicolons. The following code is a short example:

```css
body {
    font: 12px Helvetica, Arial, sans-serif;
}
a.button {
  -webkit-border-radius: 5px;
  -moz-border-radius: 5px;
  border-radius: 5px;
}
```

In Stylus, the CSS code produced may look like the following code snippet:

```stylus
body
    font 12px Helvetica, Arial, sans-serif

a.button
  -webkit-border-radius 5px
  -moz-border-radius 5px
  border-radius 5px
```

The language uses the indentation to recognize the definitions. Stylus is distributed as a Node.js module and can be installed using the `npm install -g stylus` command line. Once the process is completed, we can compile with the following command:

```
stylus ./styles.styl
```

This is the command line where `styles.styl` contains the necessary CSS. As a result, we will get the `styles.css` file in the same directory.

Stylus is a little bit more advanced than Less. It still supports the same features but has more logical operators. Let's see an example that demonstrates most of its features:

```
brandColor = #FF993D
borderSettings = { size: 3px, side: '-top' }

paragraph-border(size, side = '')
  if size > 2px
    border{side}: dotted size #999
  else
    border{side}: solid size #999

body
  font-size: 20px
  p
    color: brandColor
    paragraph-border(borderSettings.size, borderSettings.side)
```

The first line defines a variable called `brandColor`. Later, this variable is used to set the color of the paragraph. Stylus supports hash objects as a value of the variables. It's really nice because we can define a set of options. In the preceding example, `borderSettings` holds the size and the position of the paragraph's border. The `paragraph-border` mixin accepts two arguments. The second one is not mandatory and has a default value. There is an `if-else` statement that defines the type of the applied border. Similar to Less, we have the ability to nest selectors. The paragraph's styles are nested inside the `body` selector. After the compilation, the resulted CSS is as follows:

```
body {
  font-size: 20px;
}
body p {
  color: #ff993d;
  border-top: dotted 3px #999;
}
```

Working with AbsurdJS

AbsurdJS is another CSS preprocessor available in Node.js that takes a slightly different direction. Instead of inventing a new syntax, it uses the already existing language—JavaScript. So, features such as variables, mixins, or logical operators came naturally without any additional effort.

Similar to the other preprocessors, AbsurdJS is distributed via the package manager of Node.js. The following command line installs the library on your machine:

```
npm install -g absurd
```

The CSS styles are written in the .js files. In fact, the library accepts the .css, .json, and .yaml files and successfully processes them, but in this book we will stick to the JavaScript format because it is the most interesting one. Every file which is passed to AbsurdJS starts with the following code:

```
module.exports = function(api) {
    // ...
}
```

The function that is exported accepts the API of the module. All the operations work through the API object. Because everything is in JavaScript, the CSS styles are represented in the JSON format. The following is an example code:

```
module.exports = function(api) {
    api.add({
        body: {
            fontSize: '20px',
            margin: '0 12px'
        }
    })
}
```

The code is compiled to the following CSS:

```
body {
    font-size: 20px;
    margin: 0 12px;
}
```

AbsurdJS could work as a command-line tool. To process a styles.js file containing the preceding code snippet, we should execute the following code:

```
absurd -s ./styles.js -o ./styles.css
```

The -s flag comes from the source and -o from the output. The module can be used in code as well as to integrate AbsurdJS into every Node.js application. All we have to do is add the library in our package.json file and require it as shown in the following code:

```
var absurd = require('absurd')();
absurd.add({
    body: {
```

```
      fontSize: '20px',
      marginTop: '10px'
    }
}).compile(function(err, css) {
    // ...
});
```

Actually, the same thing is valid for the Less preprocessor. It could be used in a Node.js script too.

While discussing Sass and Stylus, we used an example: a few lines of code that put a border on the page's `paragraph` tag. The following code elaborates how this can be achieved using AbsurdJS:

```
module.exports = function(api) {
  var brandColor = '#993f99';
  var paragraphBorder = function(size, side) {
    var side = side ? side : '-top';
    var result = {};
    result['border' + side] = (size > 2 ? 'dotted ' : 'solid ') + size
+ 'px #999';
    return result;
  }
  api.add({
    body: {
      fontSize: '20px',
      p: [
        { color: brandColor },
        paragraphBorder(3, '-left')
      ]
    }
  });
}
```

It's all about constructing JavaScript objects and passing them to the `add` method. There is still nesting, defining variables, and using a mixin (`paragraphBorder`).

Styling a simple login form

We will now write the CSS styles for a simple login form. The HTML markup is pretty simple. It has two labels, two input fields, and two buttons, as shown in the following code:

```
<form method="post" id="login">
    <label>Your username</label>
```

```
      <input type="text" name="u" />
      <label>Your password</label>
      <input type="password" name="p" />
      <input type="submit" value="login" />
      <input type="button" value="forgot" />
   </form>
```

The result that we want to achieve at the end looks like the following screenshot:

As a preprocessor, we are going to use AbsurdJS and write our styles in the JavaScript format. Let's create an empty style.js file and enter the following code:

```
module.exports = function(api) {
   var textColor = '#9E9E9E';
   var textColorLight = api.lighten('#9E9E9E', 50);
   var textColorDark = api.darken('#9E9E9E', 50);
   var brandColor = '#8DB7CD';
   var brandColorLight = api.lighten('#8DB7CD', 50);
   var brandColorDark = api.darken('#8DB7CD', 30);
   var warning = '#F00';
}
```

We defined the settings of the page. They are only colors in our case, but it could be anything else, for example, font size, margin, or the space between the lines. The api.lighten and api.darken functions are used to produce variants of colors. They change the passed values by making them lighter or darker depending on the percentages.

We have our configurations set up and we can continue with the following basic CSS:

```
api.add({
  body: {
    width: '100%', height: '100%',
    margin: 0, padding: 0,
    color: textColor,
    fontFamily: 'Arial'
  }
});
```

These styles are applied to the `body` tag of our page. If we open the page now, we will see the following result:

This is because we have still not worked on the form. Let's continue and define the basic rules for it, using the following code:

```
api.add({
  body: {
    width: '100%', height: '100%',
    margin: 0, padding: 0,
    color: textColor,
    fontFamily: 'Arial',
    '#login': [
      {
        width: '400px',
        margin: '0 auto',
        padding: '30px 0 0 30px',
        label: {
          display: 'block',
          margin: '0 0 10px 0',
          color: textColorDark
        }
      }
    ]
  }
});
```

The #login selector matches the form. We position it in the middle of the page and set padding from the top and bottom sides. We are also making the label tag a block element. Now the example looks much better, as shown in the following screenshot:

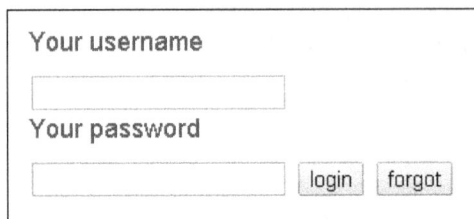

If we check the HTML markup, which we started from, we will see that the rest of the elements are the input tags, that is, two fields and two buttons. Let's create a function (mixin), which will generate CSS for these elements:

```javascript
var input = function(selector, addons) {
  var result = {};
  result[selector] = {
    '-wm-border-radius': '4px',
    '-wm-box-sizing': 'border-box',
    marginBottom: '20px',
    border: 'solid 3px ' + brandColor,
    width: '100%',
    padding: '8px',
    '&:focus': {
      outline: 0,
      background: textColorLight
    }
  }
  if(addons) {
    for(var prop in addons) {
      result[selector][prop] = addons[prop];
    }
  }
  return result;
}
```

The input method accepts a selector and an object. Because we will use the function to style fields and at the same buttons, we need a mechanism to add custom rules. The addons object (if defined) holds those styles which need to be set in addition. There are two properties that may look strange: -wm-border-radius and -wm-box-sizing. The -wm- property, at the beginning, adds browser prefixes to the end CSS. For example, -wm-box-sizing: border-box produces the following output:

```
box-sizing: border-box;
-webkit-box-sizing: border-box;
-moz-box-sizing: border-box;
```

The `&:focus` property is also a special property. The ampersand represents the selector in which the style is written. At the end of the function, we added the custom CSS. Now, let's see the use case:

```
'#login': [
  {
    width: '400px',
    margin: '0 auto',
    padding: '30px 0 0 30px',
    label: {
      display: 'block',
      margin: '0 0 10px 0',
      color: textColorDark
    }
  },
  input('input[type="text"]'),
  input('input[type="password"]', {
    marginBottom: '40px'
  }),
  input('input[type="submit"]', {
    gradient: brandColorLight + '/' + brandColor,
    width: '80px'
  }),
  input('input[type="button"]', {
    gradient: brandColorLight + '/' + brandColor,
    width: '80px',
    transparent: 0.6,
    '&:hover': {
      transparent: 1
    }
  })
]
```

For the input fields, we call the input method with only a selector. However, for the buttons, we need more styles and they are passed as a JavaScript object. AbsurdJS has built-in mixins that allow us to generate cross-browser CSS, for example, the `gradient` and `transparent` properties. The result of the execution of the `gradient` property is:

```
/* gradient: brandColorLight + '/' + brandColor */
background: -webkit-linear-gradient(0deg, #d4ffff 0%, #8DB7CD 100%);
```

```
background: -moz-linear-gradient(0deg, #d4ffff 0%, #8DB7CD 100%);
background: -ms-linear-gradient(0deg, #d4ffff 0%, #8DB7CD 100%);
background: -o-linear-gradient(0deg, #d4ffff 0%, #8DB7CD 100%);
background: linear-gradient(0deg, #d4ffff 0%, #8DB7CD 100%);
-ms-filter: progid:DXImageTransform.Microsoft.gradient
(startColorstr='#FF8DB7CD',endColorstr='#FFD4FFFF',
GradientType=0);
```

Also, the result of the execution of the `transparent` property is as follows:

```
/* transparent: 0.6  */
filter: alpha(opacity=60);
-ms-filter: progid:DXImageTransform.Microsoft.Alpha(Opacity=60);
opacity: 0.6;
-moz-opacity: 0.6;
-khtml-opacity: 0.6;
```

Using a mixin is much easier than writing all these things by ourselves. Once we add the `input` invocations, we are done. AbsurdJS produces the desired result.

Summary

CSS is and will always be an important part of the Web. Making it simple, well-structured, and with a flexible markup leads to a good architecture. In this chapter, we learned about the most popular concept to write modular CSS. Along with that, we checked the latest trends in CSS preprocessing, the available tools, and their features.

Node.js is fast and is very often used as a REST API. In the next chapter, we will see how to write a REST API and what the best practices in this direction are.

11
Writing a REST API

In the previous chapter, we learned how to optimize our CSS writing. We learned about the most popular architectural concepts and checked out the available CSS preprocessors. This chapter is about building a REST API with Node.js. We are going to:

- Run a web server
- Implement routing mechanisms
- Process the incoming requests
- Send a proper response

Discovering REST and API

REST stands for **Representational State Transfer** and it is an architectural principle of the Web. In most of the cases, we have resources on the server that need to be created, fetched, updated, or deleted. The REST APIs provide mechanisms to perform all these operations. Every resource has its own URI and based on the request method, a different action occurs. For example, let's say that we need to manage the users in our social network. To retrieve information about a specific user, we will perform the GET request to the /user/23 address, where the number, 23, is the ID of the user. To update the data, we will send the PUT request to the same URL, and to delete the record, we'll send the DELETE request. The POST requests are reserved to create new resources. In other words, the resources' management on the server happens via HTTP requests sent to carefully selected addresses by using the GET, POST, PUT, and DELETE methods, which are very often called **HTTP verbs**. A lot of companies adopt this architecture because it is simple, works through the HTTP protocol, and is highly scalable. There are, of course, different approaches such as SOAP or CORBA but we have many more rules to follow and the communication between the machines is very often complicated.

According to Wikipedia, an **Application Programming Interface (API)** specifies how some software components should interact with each other. The API is usually the part of our program that is visible to the outside world.

In this chapter, we will build one. It's an API of a simple online books library. The resources are the books and they will be accessed through the REST API.

Developing an online library – a REST API

The development of a REST API is the same as the development of every other Node.js application. We need to plan it and carefully implement the different components one by one.

Defining the API parts

It's always good to have a plan before starting a new project. So, let's define the main parts of the API server as follows:

- **Router**: We know that Node.js starts listening on a port and accepts an HTTP requests. So, we need a class that will handle them and pass the request to the right logic.
- **Handler**: This is the place where our logic will be put in. It will process the request and prepare the response.
- **Responder**: We also need a class that will send the result to the browser. Very often the API has to respond in different formats. For example, XML and, at the same time, JSON.

Writing the base

Node.js is very often used to build REST APIs. Also, because it is a common task, we have several possible approaches. There are even ready-to-use modules such as rest.js or restify. However, we are going to build our REST API from scratch because it will be much more interesting and challenging. We will start by running a Node.js server. Let's create an empty directory and put the following code into the index.js file:

```
var http = require('http');
var router = function(req, res) {
  res.end('API response');
}
http.createServer(router).listen('9000', '127.0.0.1');
console.log('API listening');
```

If we run the script with `node ./index.js`, we will be able to open `http://127.0.0.1:9000` and see **API response** on the screen. All the incoming requests are going through a function. That's the place for our router.

Implementing the API router

In almost every web-based Node.js application, the router plays one of the main roles. That's because it is the entry point of the program. That's the place where the URL is mapped to logic and the request is processed. The router for the REST API should be a little bit more advanced, because it should handle not only the usual `GET` and `POST` requests but also `PUT` and `DELETE`. Along with our `index.js`, we need another file called `router.js`. So, add the following code to the `router.js` file:

```
var routes = [];
module.exports = {
  register: function(method, route, handler) {
    routes.push({ method: method, route: route, handler:
      handler });
  },
  process: function(req, res, next) {
    // ...
  }
}
```

The module exports an object with two methods. The first one (`register`) stores records in the `routes` variable. The second method (`process`) will be used as a handler of the `createServer` method in `index.js`. The following code demonstrates how our router is used:

```
var http = require('http');
var router = require('./router');
http.createServer(router.process).listen('9000', '127.0.0.1');
console.log('API listening');
```

The first parameter of the `register` method will be the HTTP verbs as a string: `GET`, `POST`, `PUT`, or `DELETE`. The `route` parameter will be a regular expression and, the last one, a function will be called if the expression matches the current URL.

The `process` method will do several things. It will run the defined regular expression against the current request. It will also do few more things, which are as follows:

- Fetching the `GET` parameters from the URL
- Fetching the `POST`/`PUT` parameters passed with the request
- Supporting dynamic URLs

All these mentioned things could be implemented outside the `router` variable but because they are common tasks and we will probably have them in several places, we will add them in the following code. The following code is the full code of the router's `process` method:

```
process: function(req, res, next) {
    var urlInfo = url.parse(req.url, true);
    var info = {
        get: urlInfo.query,
        post: {},
        path: urlInfo.pathname,
        method: req.method
    }
    for(var i=0; i<routes.length; i++) {
        var r = routes[i];
        var match = info.path.match(r.route);
        if((info.method === r.method || '' === r.method) && match) {
            info.match = match;
            if(info.method === 'POST' || info.method === 'PUT') {
                processRequest(req, function(body) {
                    info.post = body;
                    r.handler(req, res, info);
                });
            } else {
                r.handler(req, res, info);
            }
            return;
        }
    }
    res.end('');
}
```

There is an `info` object holding the data which we talked about. We cycled over all the routes and tried to find one which has method and regular expression matching. We also checked if the request method is POST or PUT and got the sent information. At the end, if there is no matching route, we send an empty string. To get the preceding code working, we need to define two variables and one function, which are done in the following code:

```
var url = require('url');
var qs = require('querystring');
var processRequest = function(req, callback) {
    var body = '';
    req.on('data', function (data) {
```

```
        body += data;
    });
    req.on('end', function () {
        callback(qs.parse(body));
    });
}
```

The entities, `url` and `querystring`, are native Node.js modules. The `processRequest` variable is needed because Node.js handles the POST/PUT parameters differently.

By using the preceding code, we are able to add routes and check if they work properly. For example, see the following code in the `index.js` file:

```
router.register('GET', /\/books(.+)?/, function(req, res, info) {
    console.log(info);
    res.end('Getting all the books')
});
```

Here, we run the server with `node ./index.js` and fire a request to `http://127.0.0.1:9000/books`. The result is a text `Getting all the books` on the screen, as shown in the following screenshot:

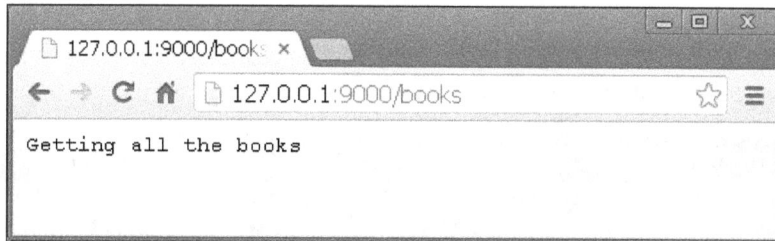

You will also see the following output in our terminal:

```
{ get: {},
  post: {},
  path: '/books',
  method: 'GET',
  match: [ '/books', undefined, index: 0, input: '/books' ] }
```

There is no sent data so the `get` and `post` properties are empty. Now, let's use the following route:

```
router.register('POST', /\/book(.+)?/, function(req, res, info) {
    console.log(info);
    res.end('New book created')
});
```

We should make sure that our API accepts the POST and GET requests properly; we can do that by using this route. If we send a POST request with the data name=Node. js blueprints&author=Krasimir Tsonev to the http://127.0.0.1:9000/ book?notification=no URL, we will get the following result:

```
{ get: { notification: 'no' },
  post: { name: 'Node.js blueprints', author: 'Krasimir Tsonev' },
  path: '/book',
  method: 'POST',
  match: [ '/book', undefined, index: 0, input: '/book' ] }
```

There is one more thing that our router does. It handles dynamic URLs. By *dynamic*, we mean URLs such as /book/523/edit, where 523 is the unique ID of the book and it can be something different and we want to process all requests of this type in one specific handler as follows:

```
router.register('GET', /\/book\/(.+)\/(.+)?/,
    function(req, res, info) {
    console.log(info);
    res.end('Getting specific book')
});
```

The key moment here is the regular expression. There are two capturing parentheses. The first one represents the ID of the book and the second one, the action that we want to perform. For example, edit or delete. The response of 127.0.0.1:9000/ book/523/edit is as shown in the following screenshot:

```
{ get: {},
  post: {},
  path: '/book/523/edit',
  method: 'GET',
  match:
   [ '/book/523/edit',
     '523',
     'edit',
     index: 0,
     input: '/book/523/edit' ] }
```

As we can see, 523 and edit are a part of the match property and we can get them easily. We can improve our router by adding a few additional helper methods. It's a good practice to provide methods for every different type of request. The following code shows how these methods look like:

```
get: function(route, handler) {
    this.register('GET', route, handler);
},
post: function(route, handler) {
```

```
        this.register('POST', route, handler);
    },
    put: function(route, handler) {
        this.register('PUT', route, handler);
    },
    del: function(route, handler) {
        this.register('DELETE', route, handler);
    },
    all: function(route, handler) {
        this.register('', route, handler);
    }
```

Instead of `router.register('GET', /\/book\/(.+)\/(.+)?/...`, we can now write `router.get(/\/book\/(.+)\/(.+)?/...`, which is a little bit better. The `all` function could be used if we need to handle a specific URL but don't care about the `request` method. The same approach is used in the Express framework, where we have the `get`, `post`, `put`, `delete`, and `all` methods.

Writing the responder

Before writing the logic of our little REST API library, we need a proper responder, that is, a class which we will use to send the result to the browser. There is something really important that we need to take care of while we are talking about a server which works as an API. Along with the data, we have to send a proper status code. For example, `200` if everything is fine or `404` if the resource is missing.

Our responder will be saved in the `responder.js` file located in the same directory as `index.js` and `router.js`. The module starts with the following code:

```
module.exports = function(res) {
    return {
        c: 200,
        code: function(c) {
            this.c = c;
            return this;
        },
        send: function(content) {
            res.end(content.toString('utf8'));
            this.c = 200;
            return this;
        }
    }
}
```

The module requires the response object in order to send the result to the browser. The `code` method sets the status code. We can get the latest used route and transform it to the following code:

```
var responder = require('./responder');
router.get(/\/book\/(.+)\/(.+)?/, function(req, res, info) {
  console.log(info);
  responder(res).code(200).send('Getting specific book');
});
```

At the beginning of this chapter, we said that the API should be able to respond in different formats. We have to add a few methods in the responder to make this possible:

```
json: function(o) {
  res.writeHead(this.c, {'Content-Type':
    'application/json; charset=utf-8'});
  return this.send(JSON.stringify(o));
},
html: function(content) {
  res.writeHead(this.c, {'Content-Type': 'text/html;
    charset=utf-8'});
  return this.send(content);
},
css: function(content) {
  res.writeHead(this.c, {'Content-Type': 'text/css;
    charset=utf-8'});
  return this.send(content);
},
js: function(content) {
  res.writeHead(this.c, {'Content-Type': '
    application/javascript; charset=utf-8'});
  return this.send(content);
},
text: function(content) {
  res.writeHead(this.c, {'Content-Type':
    'text/plain; charset=utf-8'});
  return this.send(content);
}
```

By adding these functions, we are actually able to serve JSON, HTML, CSS, JavaScript, and plain text. The class sends a header to the browser specifying the status code, `Content-Type` and `charset`. All the methods of the responder return the class itself, so we can chain them.

Working with the database

In *Chapter 3, Writing a Blog Application with Node.js and AngularJS*, we used MongoDB and MySQL. We learned how to read, write, edit, and delete records from these databases. Let's use MongoDB in this chapter, too. We will store our data in a collection named books. To use the database driver, we need to create a package.json file and put the following content in it:

```
{
  "name": "projectname",
  "description": "description",
  "version": "0.0.1",
  "dependencies": {
    "mongodb": "1.3.20"
    "request": "2.34.0"

  }
}
```

After running npm install, we will be able to connect to the MongoDB server by using the driver installed in the node_modules directory. The code that we need to interact with the database is the same as the one used in *Chapter 3, Writing a Blog Application with Node.js and AngularJS*, which is as follows:

```
var crypto = require("crypto"),
    client = require('mongodb').MongoClient,
  mongodb_host = "127.0.0.1",
  mongodb_port = "27017",
  collection;

var connection = 'mongodb://';
connection += mongodb_host + ':' + mongodb_port;
connection += '/library';
client.connect(connection, function(err, database) {
  if(err) {
    throw new Error("Can't connect.");
  } else {
    console.log("Connection to MongoDB server successful.");
      collection = database.collection('books');
    }
});
```

The crypto module will be used to generate a unique ID for the newly created records. There is a MongoDB client initialized. It is connected to the server and makes the collection variable point to the books collection. That's all we need. We can now manage records of our books.

Creating a new record

The adding of a new book into the database should happen via the POST request. The following code is the route that will handle this task:

```
router.post(/\/book/, function(req, res, info) {
  var book = info.post;
  book.ID = crypto.randomBytes(20).toString('hex');
  if(typeof book.name == 'undefined') {
    responder(res).code(400).json({error: 'Missing name.'});
  } else if(typeof book.author == 'undefined') {
    responder(res).code(400).json({error: 'Missing author.'});
  } else {
    collection.insert(book, {}, function() {
      responder(res).code(201.json({message:
        'Record created successful.'});
    });
  }
});
```

The URL to add a new book is /book. It can be accessed via the POST method. The expected parameters are name and author. Notice that we are setting the status code as 400 if any of these are missing. 400 means Bad request. If the user forgets to pass them, we should notify him or her of what exactly is wrong. This is really important while designing an API. The developers who use our services should know why they didn't get the proper response. Very often, the well designed APIs could be used without documentation. That's because their methods provide enough information.

The book's data is written in the JSON format and the answer to the browser is also sent in the JSON format. The following screenshot is a preview of the record saved in the database:

```
{
  "name": "Test Book",
  "author": "Test Author",
  "ID": "90d426331f82e744aadc89d5ba6678656e846a3c",
  "_id": ObjectId("533c6e62ccb774d41f4f52f2")
}
```

Editing a record

To implement editing, we will use the PUT method. We will also need to define a dynamic route. The following code creates the route and the proper handler:

```
router.put(/\/book\/(.+)?/, function(req, res, info) {
  var book = info.post;
  if(typeof book.name === 'undefined') {
    responder(res).code(400).json({error: 'Missing name.'});
  } else if(typeof book.author === 'undefined') {
    responder(res).code(400).json({error: 'Missing author.'});
  } else {
    var ID = info.match[1];
    collection.find({ID: ID}).toArray(function(err, records) {
      if(records && records.length > 0) {
        book.ID = ID;
        collection.update({ID: ID}, book, {}, function() {
          responder(res).code(200).json({message:
            'Record updated successful.'});
        });
      } else {
        responder(res).code(400).json({error: 'Missing record.'});
      }
    });
  }
});
```

Along with the checks for missing name and author, we need to make sure that the ID that is used in the URL exists in our database. If not, a proper error message should be sent.

Deleting a record

The deletion of records is really similar to the editing. We will again need a dynamic route. When we have the ID of the book, we can check if it really exists and if yes, simply remove it from the database. Checkout the following implementation that does the actions that we just described:

```
router.del(/\/book\/(.+)?/, function(req, res, info) {
  var ID = info.match[1];
  collection.find({ID: ID}).toArray(function(err, records) {
    if(records && records.length > 0) {
      collection.findAndModify({ID: ID}, [], {},
        {remove: true}, function() {
```

```
        responder(res).code(200).json({message:
          'Record removed successfully.'});
      });
  } else {
    responder(res).code(400).json({error: 'Missing record.'});
  }
  });
});
```

Displaying all the books

This is maybe the simplest API method, which we will have to implement. There is a query to the database and the result is directly passed to the responder. The following code defines a route books that fetches all the records from the database:

```
router.get(/\/books/, function(req, res, info) {
  collection.find({}).toArray(function(err, records) {
    if(!err) {
      responder(res).code(200).json(records);
    } else {
      responder(res).code(200).json([]);
    }
  });
});
```

Adding a default route

We should have a default route, that is, a page that will be sent if the user types in a wrong URL or just visits the root address of the API. In order to catch every type of request, we use the all method of the router:

```
router.all('', function(req, res, info) {
  var html = '';
  html += 'Available methods:<br />';
  html += '<ul>';
  html += '<li>GET /books</li>';
  html += '<li>POST /book</li>';
  html += '<li>PUT /book/[id]</li>';
  html += '<li>DELETE /book/[id]</li>';
  html += '</ul>';
  responder(res).code(200).html(html);
});
```

We constructed a simple HTML markup and sent it to the user. The route's regular expression is just an empty string, which matches everything. We are also using the .all function, which handles any type of request. Notice that we need to add this route after all the others; otherwise, if it is at the start, all the requests will go there.

Testing the API

To make sure that everything works, we will write a few tests covering all the methods mentioned in the previous sections. In *Chapter 9*, *Automate Your Testing with Node.js*, we learned about Jasmine and Mocha test frameworks. The following test suite uses Jasmine. We will also need one additional module to make HTTP requests. The module is called request and we can get it using npm install request or by adding it to our package.json file. The following are the steps along with the code to test the API:

1. Let's first test the creation of a new database record:

```
var request = require('request');
var endpoint = 'http://127.0.0.1:9000/';
var bookID = '';
describe("Testing API", function() {
  it("should create a new book record", function(done) {
    request.post({
      url: endpoint + '/book',
      form: {
        name: 'Test Book',
        author: 'Test Author'
      }
    }, function (e, r, body) {
      expect(body).toBeDefined();
      expect(JSON.parse(body).message).toBeDefined();
      expect(JSON.parse(body).message).toBe
        ('Record created successfully.');
      done();
    });
  });
});
```

We are using the .post method of the module. The needed data is attached to a form property. Also, we expect to receive the JSON object containing a specific message.

2. To get all the books in the database, we need to perform a request to
   `http://127.0.0.1:9000/books`:

```
it("should get all the books", function(done) {
  request.get({
    url: endpoint + '/books'
  }, function (e, r, body) {
    var books = JSON.parse(body);
    expect(body).toBeDefined();
    expect(books.length > 0).toBeDefined();
    bookID = books[0].ID;
    expect(bookID).toBeDefined();
    done();
  });
});
```

3. The editing and removing operations are similar to the POST and GET
   requests except for the fact that we are passing an ID. Also, we got it from the
   last test where we fetched all the records in the collection:

```
it("should edit", function(done) {
  request.put({
    url: endpoint + '/book/' + bookID,
    form: {
      name: 'New name',
      author: 'New author'
    }
  }, function (e, r, body) {
    expect(body).toBeDefined();
    expect(JSON.parse(body).message).toBeDefined();
    expect(JSON.parse(body).message).toBe
      ('Record updated successfully.');
    done();
  });
});
it("should delete a book", function(done) {
  request.del({
    url: endpoint + '/book/' + bookID
  }, function (e, r, body) {
    expect(body).toBeDefined();
    expect(JSON.parse(body).message).toBeDefined();
    expect(JSON.parse(body).message).toBe
      ('Record removed successfully.');
    done();
  });
});
```

Summary

In this chapter, we built a REST API to store information about books. Node.js handles such tasks well because it has easy-to-work native modules. We successfully covered the GET, POST, PUT, and DELETE requests that created an interface to manage a simple online library.

In the next and last chapter of this book, we will build a desktop application. We will learn how Node.js can be used not only for web projects, but for desktop programs too. By the end of the next chapter, we should have a working file browser written with Node.js.

12

Developing Desktop Apps with Node.js

In the previous chapter, we implemented a REST API and built a server that processes various requests. Most of the chapters in this book present web technologies, applications that work in a browser with the HTTP protocol. It's interesting that Node.js can be used to produce desktop programs, and we don't have to learn a new language or use a new tool. We can continue using HTML, CSS, and JavaScript. This is a great benefit because these technologies are easy to learn and develop. Node.js is also really fast: We save a lot of time when dealing with large amounts of written modules because we don't have to deal with trivial problems. In this chapter, we will write a file browser. Our application will perform the following:

- Run as a desktop program
- Read the files from our hard drive and display them on the screen
- Display images

Using node-webkit

There are several tools available to write desktop apps. We will use node-webkit (`https://github.com/rogerwang/node-webkit`). It's an app runtime based on Chromium and Node.js. It's distributed as a binary program we run to see the result of our code. It is available for all the major operating systems — Linux, Windows, and Mac. So during the development, we will use the `nw` executable file, which is the same as using the `node` executable to run Node.js scripts. The `nw` file can be downloaded from the official repository of the tool in GitHub.

Every desktop application written with node-webkit must contain at least two files: `package.json` and the main HTML file. Similar to the modules we wrote so far, the `package.json` file holds the configuration of our application. The following is a simple example:

```
{
    "name": "nw-demo",
    "main": "index.html"
}
```

It's important that we set a value for the `main` property. It should point to the main HTML file of our file browser. The path is relative to the location of the `package.json` file. The content of `index.html` will be something like the following:

```
<!DOCTYPE html>
<html>
  <head>
    <title>Hello World!</title>
  </head>
  <body>
    <h1>Hello World!</h1>
    We are using node.js
      <script>document.write(process.version)</script>.
  </body>
</html>
```

This is just a regular HTML page, except for the code placed between the `script` tags. The `document.write` method is available in every modern browser. However, `process` is a Node.js global object. The example is a simple one, but we can see the power of node-webkit. In practice, we can mix the client-side JavaScript with a server-side JavaScript, which is run in the context of our machine. We can code like we do in the Node.js environment while still having access to the DOM of the page.

The following are two ways to run the app:

- We can navigate to the directory that contains the files and run `nw ./`
- We can zip the two files to `myapp.zip` for example, rename the archive to `myapp.nw`, and run `nw myapp.nw`

Once we are done programming, we can pack it along with the node-webkit executable. For end-users, this means not having to install additional software or download node-webkit separately. This makes the distribution much easier. There are some rules that we as developers should follow, for example, ship few `.dll` file (under Windows OS) and license files. However, it's good to know that it is possible to pack the project and run it on other machines without installing dependencies.

The steps to do this depend on the operating system and are well-defined in the official documentation (`https://github.com/rogerwang/node-webkit`). As mentioned, node-webkit is based on Chromium. Generally, when we write a client-side JavaScript or CSS, we deal with a lot of problems because there are differences between the browsers. However, here we have only one browser and don't have to think about tricky workarounds. All we have to do is write code that works under Webkit. We can also use almost the same developer tools panel that we have in Google Chrome. After launching our application, we will see the following window— that is, a window produced by node-webkit:

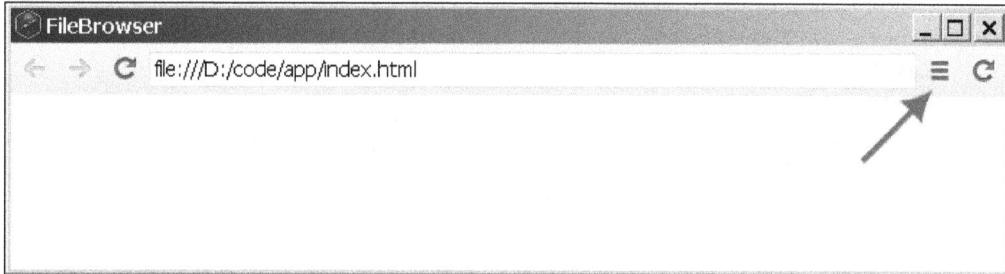

There is a small button in the upper-right corner, which gives us access to the **Elements**, **Network**, **Sources**, **Timeline**, **Profiles**, **Resources**, **Audits**, and **Console** panels. When we click the button we will see a window like the one in the following screenshot:

Having the same instruments simplifies the debugging and testing processes. As we pointed out at the beginning of this chapter, we don't have to learn a new language or use different technologies. We can stick to the usual HTML, CSS, and JavaScript.

Writing the base of the application

Before starting the actual implementation of our file browser, we must prepare the HTML layout, the base of the JavaScript part, and the `package.json` file.

Writing the package.json file

The `package.json` file should be placed in the main path of the project. It's a file with content similar to the following code:

```
{
  "name": "FileBrowser",
  "main": "index.html",
  "window": {
    "toolbar": true,
    "width": 1024,
    "height": 800
  }
}
```

We already discussed the `name` and `main` properties. The `window` object is a desktop-specific setting; it tells node-webkit how the main application's window should look. In the preceding code, we set only three properties. The `width` and `height` properties defines the window size and `toolbar` hides or shows the uppermost panel, the one that makes our program look like a browser. Usually, we don't need it and at the end of the development cycle, we set `toolbar` to `false`. There are few other options we can apply, for example, `title` or `icon`. We can even hide the close, maximize, and minimize buttons.

Preparing the HTML layout

The HTML code we start with preparing the layout is as follows:

```
<!DOCTYPE html>
<html lang="en">
    <head>
        <meta charset="utf-8">
        <title>FileBrowser</title>
        <link rel="stylesheet" href="css/styles.css">
        <link rel="stylesheet"
          href="css/font-awesome-4.0.3/css/font-awesome.min.css">
        <script src="js/scripts.js"></script>
    </head>
    <body>
```

```
<section class="tree-area">
  <div class="current-location"></div>
  <div class="tree"></div>
</section>
  <section class="file-info"></section>
</body>
</html>
```

There are two CSS files. The first one, `styles.css`, contains the styles written specifically for our application and the second one, uses the cool font icons from `font-awesome`, icons that are represented by a font and not an image. The exact content of this resource is not included in this chapter, but you can find it in the additional material provided with the book.

Also, a `scripts.js` file will host the JavaScript logic of the file browser.

The application has the following two parts:

- **tree**: This is where we will show the current directory's name and its content (files and folders)
- **file info**: If a file is selected, this area will show some of its characteristics and the buttons to copy, move, and delete

If we run node-webkit with the preceding code, the result will be as follows:

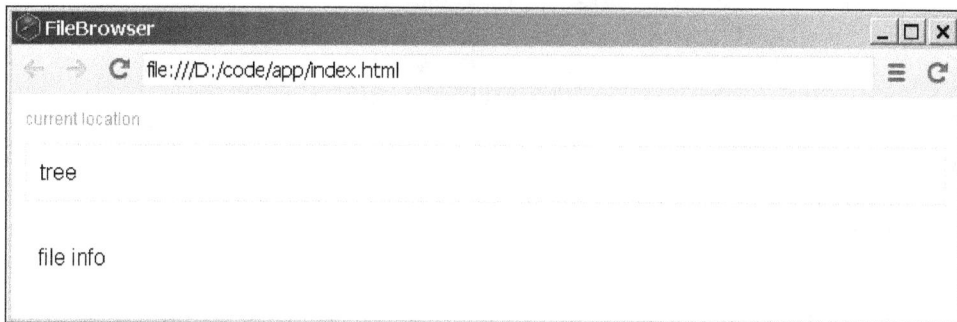

Designing the JavaScript base

Let's open the `scripts.js` file and see how to structure the JavaScript code. At the beginning of the file, we define the required Node.js modules and a global variable, `root`:

```
var fs = require('fs');
var path = require('path');
var root = path.normalize(process.cwd());
```

We use the `fs` module for all filesystem-related operations. The `path` module contains utility methods used to work with file paths. There are some differences between the operating systems for example, in Windows, the paths are written with a backslash, whereas in Linux, it uses a forward slash. The `path.normalize` method takes care of this by correcting the string to it proper format depending on the OS.

The first folder we are going to read will be the directory the application is started in. Thus, we are use `process.cwd()` to get the current working directory.

It's not a good practice to work in the global scope, so we will create a JavaScript class called `Tree` using the following code:

```
var Tree = function() {

  var api = {},
      el,
      currentLocationArea,
      treeArea,
      fileArea

  api.cwd = root;
  api.csf = null;

  api.init = function(selector) {
    el = document.querySelector(selector);
    currentLocationArea = el.querySelector('.current-location');
    treeArea = el.querySelector('.tree');
    fileArea = document.querySelector('.file-info');
    return api;
  }

  return api;
}
```

The definition in the preceding code uses the revealing module pattern, which is a great pattern to encapsulate the JavaScript logic. The `api` object is the public interface of the class and is returned at the end. The variables `el`, `currentLocationArea`, `treeArea`, and `fileArea` are private variables and represent the DOM elements on the page. They are initialized in the `init` method. It's a good practice to cache the queries to the DOM. By storing the elements' references in local variables, we avoid the additional `querySelector` calls.

There are two public properties: `cwd` (current working directory) and `csf` (current selected file). We make them public because we may need them outside the module. In the beginning, there is no selected file and the value of `csf` is `null`.

Similar to the development in the browser, we need an entry point. Our code is run in Chromium, so using `window.onload` looks like a good choice. We will put our initializing code inside the `onload` handler as follows:

```
var FileBrowser;
window.onload = function() {
   FileBrowser = Tree().init('.tree-area');
}
```

We simply create an instance of our class and call the `init` method. We are passing the `.tree-area` parameter, the selector of the `<section>` tag, which will display the files.

Displaying and using the working directory

In this section, we will cover the main features of our file browser. At the end, our application will read the current working directory. It will show its content and the user will be able to navigate between the shown folders.

Displaying the current working directory

We put the value of `api.cwd` in the div with the `currentLocation` class. It is represented by the `currentLocationArea` private variable. We only need a function that sets the `innerHTML` property of the element:

```
var updateCurrentLocation = function() {
   currentLocationArea.innerHTML = api.cwd;
}
```

This is probably the simplest function of our class. We will call it every time we change the directory, which can happen pretty often. It's a good idea to delegate this calling to another method. Along with updating the current location area, we will refresh the files area too. So, it makes sense to write a `render` function. At the moment, the method calls only `updateCurrentLocation`, but we will add more functions later:

```
var render = function() {
   updateCurrentLocation();
}
api.init = function(selector) {
   ...
   render();
   return api;
}
```

Of course, we should call this `render` function inside the `init` method, which gives us the result as follows:

Note that now our file browser shows the directory where the process starts from.

Showing the files and folders

In this part of the chapter, we will create a function that shows all the files and folders placed inside the current working directory. This may sound like an excellent feature, but it comes with its own problems. The major one is if we go to the root of our filesystem, we have to show a large number of the items on the screen. So, instead of building a giant tree, we will stop at the third level of nesting. Let's add two new private variables:

```
var html = '';
var maxLevels = 3;
```

The `html` variable will keep the string we apply to the `innerHTML` property of the `treeArea` element.

Our browser will process the files and the directories differently. If the user selects a file, then it should display information about it such as when was the file created, its size, and so on. Along with that our program will provide few buttons for operations such as copying, moving, or deleting the file. If a folder is clicked, then the `api.cwd` variable should be changed and the `render` method should be fired. The visual representation should also be different. The following function will add a new item to the tree:

```
var addItem = function(itemPath, fullPath, isFile, indent) {
  itemPath = path.normalize(itemPath).replace(root, '');
  var calculateIndent = function() {
    var tab = '    ', str = '';
    for(var i=0; i<indent; i++) {
      str += tab;
    }
```

```
      return str;
    }
    if(isFile) {
      html += '<a href="#" class="file"
        data-path="' + fullPath + '">';
      html += calculateIndent(indent) +
        '<i class="fa fa-file-o"></i> ' + itemPath + '</a>';
    } else {
      html += '<a href="#" class="dir"
        data-path="' + fullPath + '">';
      html += calculateIndent(indent) +
        '<i class="fa fa-folder-o"></i> ' + itemPath + '</a>';
    }
  }
}
```

The `itemPath` argument contains only the name of the file or directory, while
`fullPath` shows the absolute path to the item. Based on the `isFile` parameter, the
icon of the appended link is properly chosen. The latest `indent` argument is needed
to define the visual look of the tree. Without this, all the links will start from the
left-hand side of the window. Note that we add the full path to the file or folder in a
`data-path` attribute. We do this because later any link can be clicked and we need to
know what is selected.

Now, we need a function that uses the `addItem` function, which accepts a path and
goes through all the files and subdirectories. We also need some kind of recursive
calling of the method so that we can produce a tree. As we can see in the following
code, there is a check if we are reading directory and if yes then again the walk
function is executed:

```
var walk = function(dir, level, done) {
  if(level === maxLevels) {
    done();
    return;
  }
  fs.readdir(dir, function(err, list) {
    if (err) return done(err);
    var i = 0;
    (function next() {
        var file = list[i++];
        if(!file) return done();
      var filePath = dir + '/' + file;
      fs.stat(filePath, function(err, stat) {
          if (stat && stat.isDirectory()) {
            addItem(file, filePath, false, level);
              walk(filePath, level + 1, function() {
                next();
              });
```

```
            } else {
              if (level === 0) {
                  addItem(file, filePath, true, level);
              }
              next();
          }
        });
      })();
    });
  };
```

Because the `walk` function will be called repeatedly, we need to check whether it reaches the maximum level of nesting (which in our case is set to 3); this is the purpose of the first few lines. Immediately after, the `fs.readdir` function is called. This is an asynchronous Node.js native function that returns the content in a passed directory. In the closure, which receives the data, we will go through every result and check whether the item is a file or folder. If it is a folder, then the `walk` function is called again. Note that we are passing the level and it is incremented on every call.

At the end, we just need to run the `walk` method and populate the `html` variable with an initial value as it is done in the following code:

```
var updateFiles = function() {
  html = '<a href="#" class="dir" data-path="' +
    path.normalize(api.cwd + '/../') + '">
    <i class="fa fa-level-up"></i> ..</a>';
  walk(api.cwd, 0, function() {
    treeArea.innerHTML = html;
  });
}
```

At the top of the file's tree, we added a link that points to the parent directory. This is how the user can move upward in the filesystem.

The updated render method is as follows:

```
var render = function() {
  updateCurrentLocation();
  updateFiles();
}
```

As we can see, the `updateFiles` method is called pretty often. It's kind of an expensive process because it runs the `walk` function. This is also one of the reasons behind limiting the folder's nesting. If we launch the application now, we should see the current directory at the top of the screen and its content in the `treeArea` element. The following screenshot is how this looks on the screen:

```
 FileBrowser                                                    _ □ ×
 ←  →  C   file:///D:/code/app/index.html                      ≡  C

 d:\code\app

 ↟ ..
 ▭ css
    ▭ font-awesome-4.0.3
       ▭ css
       ▭ fonts
       ▭ less
       ▭ scss
 ▭ empty
    ▭ A
    ▭ B
 ▯ index.html
 ▭ js
 ▯ package.json


 file info
```

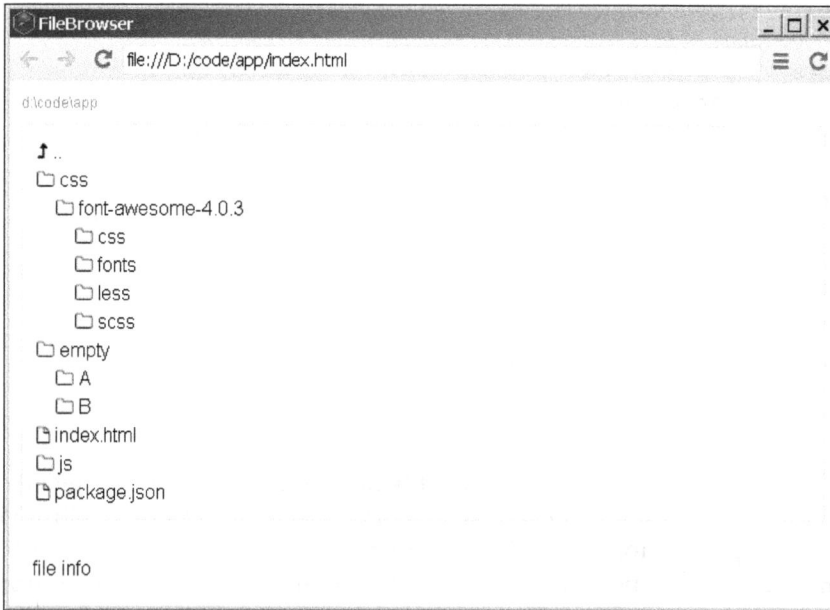

Changing the current directory

Our file browser successfully shows the files located on our hard disk. The next thing we want to do is to jump from one folder to another. Because we carefully designed our class, it is easy to implement this feature. The following two steps will change the directory:

- Update the `api.cwd` variable
- Call the `render` method

These two actions should be executed when the user clicks on some of the items in the tree. The very popular approach is to attach a `click` handler on every link and listen for user interaction. However, this will lead to some problems. We have to reassign the listeners every time the tree is updated; this is because the elements that the listeners are attached to have been replaced and are no longer in the DOM. A much better approach is to add only one handler on the `treeArea` element. When its children produce the `click` event, by default, it is bubbled upwards over the DOM. Moreover, because we do not catch it, it reaches the handler of the `treeArea` element. So the following `setEvents` function listens for the click events triggered in the `treeArea` object:

```
var setEvents = function() {
  treeArea.addEventListener('click', function(e) {
    e.preventDefault();
```

```
        if(e.target.nodeName !== 'A' && e.target.nodeName !== 'I')
          return;
        var link = e.target.nodeName === 'A' ? e.target :
          e.target.parentNode;
        var itemPath = path.normalize(link.getAttribute('data-path'));
        var isFile = link.getAttribute('class') === 'file';
        if(isFile) {
          updateFileArea(itemPath);
        } else {
          api.cwd = itemPath;
          render();
        }
      });
    }
```

The calling of `e.preventDefault` is needed because we don't want the default link behavior. The `href` attribute of all the `<a>` tags is set to #. Normally, this will scroll the page up to the top. However, we don't want this to happen, so we call `e.preventDefault`. The next check guarantees that the `click` event comes from the right element. This is actually really important because the user may click on some other element, which is still the child of `treeArea`. We expect to get the `<a>` or `<i>` (the icon inside the link) tag. The path to the file or folder is from the `data-path` attribute. To determine whether the currently selected item is a file, we check the value of its `class` attribute. On the other hand, if the user clicks on a folder, we simple trigger the `render` method; otherwise, a new function, `updateFileArea`, is called.

The function we just discussed (`setEvents`) is fired only once, and a proper place to do this is the `init` method:

```
api.init = function(selector) {
  ...
  setEvents();
  return api;
}
```

Copying, moving, and deleting files

We implemented the folder switching, and the last thing to do is file processing. We already mentioned calling the `updateFileArea` function. It should accept the file path. The following code is the body of the function:

```
var updateFileArea = function(itemPath) {
  var html = '';
  api.csf = itemPath;
```

```
if(itemPath) {
  fs.stat(itemPath, function(err, stat) {
    html += '<h3>' + path.basename(itemPath) + '</h3>';
    html += '<p>path: ' + path.dirname(itemPath) + '</p>';
    html += '<p class="small">size: ' + stat.size +
      ' bytes</p>';
    html += '<p class="small">last modified: ' +
      stat.mtime + '</p>';
    html += '<p class="small">created: ' + stat.ctime + '</p>';
    html += '<a href="javascript:FileBrowser.copy()">
      <i class="fa fa-copy"></i> Copy</a>';
    html += '<a href="javascript:FileBrowser.move()">
      <i class="fa fa-share"></i> Move</a>';
    html += '<a href="javascript:FileBrowser.del()">
      <i class="fa fa-times"></i> Delete</a>';
    fileArea.innerHTML = html;
  });
} else {
  fileArea.innerHTML = '';
}
}
```

The function of the method is to fill the `fileArea` element with information about the file. We will use the same function to clear the `fileArea` element when the user clicks on a folder. So, if `updateFileArea` is called without any parameter, the information block becomes empty. The file size and created and modified time are available because of the native Node.js function `fs.stat`. Below the file's characteristics, we place three buttons. Every button calls a method of the global `FileBrowser` object, which is an instance of our `Tree` class. Note that we do not pass the path to the file. The `copy`, `move`, and `del` functions will get this information from the `api.csf` variable that we filled earlier. The following method will be used to copy a file from one place to another:

```
api.copy = function() {
  if(!api.csf) return;
    getFolder(function(dir) {
      var file = path.basename(api.csf);
      fs.createReadStream(api.csf).pipe
        (fs.createWriteStream(dir + '/' + file));
      api.csf = null;
      updateFileArea();
      alert('File: ' + file + ' copied.');
    });
}
```

So, we know the file we want to copy, move, or delete and its absolute path. It is stored in `api.csf`. To copy and move, we need a destination path. The user should be able to pick a directory on the hard disk, and because this process occurs in two locations, it is a good idea to wrap it in a function—`getFolder`. Once this method returns the destination, we simply get the content as a stream and save it to another place. The following is the body of the `getFolder` helper:

```
var getFolder = function(callback) {
    var event = new MouseEvent('click', {
        'view': window,
        'bubbles': true,
        'cancelable': true
    });
    var input = document.createElement('INPUT');
    input.setAttribute('type', 'file');
    input.setAttribute('webkitdirectory', 'webkitdirectory');
    input.addEventListener('change', function (e) {
        callback(this.value);
    });
    input.dispatchEvent(event);
}
```

Normally, the dialog to select a directory cannot be opened without user interaction. However, in node-webkit this is possible. As we can see in the preceding code, we create a new `MouseEvent` event and a new `<input>` element to dispatch this event. The key factor here is the `webkitdirectory` attribute, which is node-webkit specific, and it transforms the element from a file selector to a folder selector. The `getFolder` function accepts a `callback` function, which is called once the user selects a directory.

The function that deletes a file looks like following code snippet:

```
api.del = function() {
    if(!api.csf) return;
    fs.unlink(api.csf, function() {
        alert('File: ' + path.basename(api.csf) + ' deleted.');
        render();
        api.csf = null;
    });
}
```

The function that deletes the file is almost the same, except that it uses `fs.unlink` to remove the file from the OS. At the end, the method that moves the file, combines both the `copy` and `del` functions.

```
api.move = function() {
    if(!api.csf) return;
    getFolder(function(dir) {
```

```
        var file = path.basename(api.csf);
        fs.createReadStream(api.csf).pipe(fs.createWriteStream(dir + '/'
  + file));
        fs.unlink(api.csf, function() {
            alert('File: ' + file + ' moved.');
            render();
            api.csf = null;
        });
    });
}
```

We need to copy the file and then delete it from the original location. With this last addition, our file browser is finished. The following screenshot shows how it looks when a file is selected:

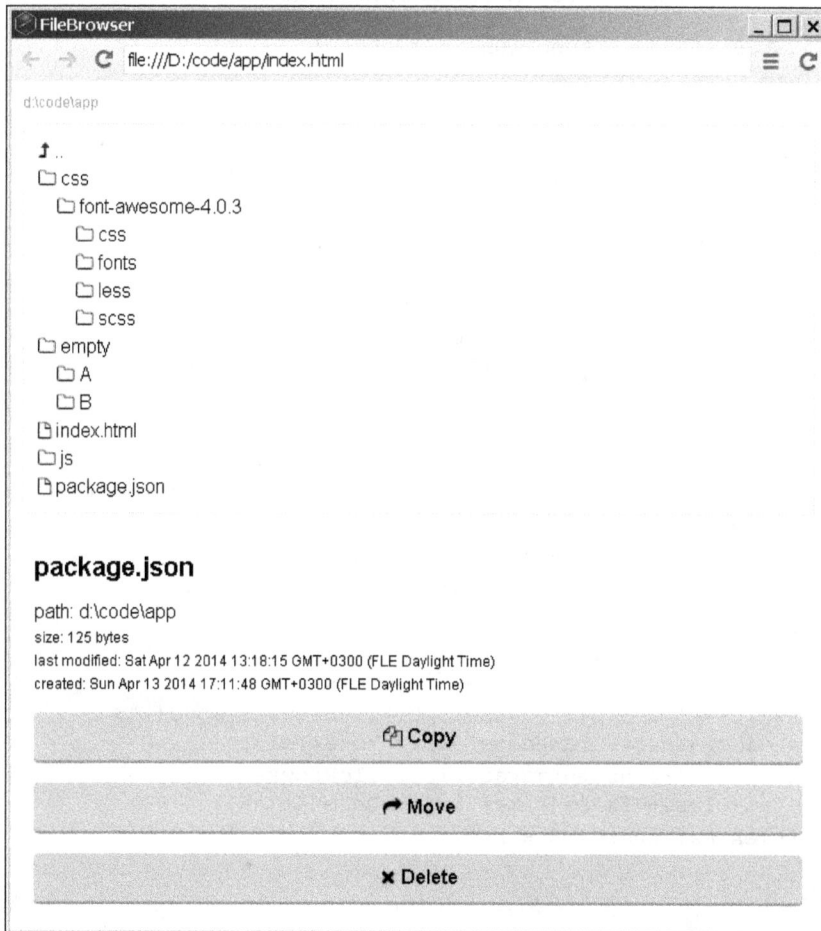

Extending the application

Our file browser looks good so far. We can see the folders and files on our machine and can copy, move, or delete them. Also, we did all this with only HTML, CSS, and JavaScript. Let's continue and add a new feature. The application we wrote is run by Chromium. In other words, our HTML and CSS are rendered by the browser, so we can easily show images in it. In the next few pages, we will create a program picture viewer.

Tweaking the updateFileArea function

The first thing to do is find out whether the currently selected file is an image. We will display the JPEG and PNG files, so we should check whether the file matches one of these extensions. Before populating the `html` variable with the markup, we will extract the file's extension as it is done in the code below:

```
var updateFileArea = function(itemPath) {
  var html = '';
  api.csf = itemPath;
  if(itemPath) {
    fs.stat(itemPath, function(err, stat) {
      var ext = path.extname(itemPath).toLowerCase();
      var isImage = ext === '.jpg' || ext ===
        '.jpeg' || ext === '.png';
      html += '<h3>' + path.basename(itemPath) + '</h3>';
      html += '<p>path: ' + path.dirname(itemPath) + '</p>';
      html += '<p class="small">size: ' + stat.size +
        ' bytes</p>';
      html += '<p class="small">last modified: ' +
        stat.mtime + '</p>';
      html += '<p class="small">created: ' + stat.ctime + '</p>';
      if(isImage) {
        html += '<a href="javascript:FileBrowser.viewImage()">
          <i class="fa fa-picture-o"></i> View image</a>';
      }
      html += '<a href="javascript:FileBrowser.copy()">
        <i class="fa fa-copy"></i> Copy</a>';
      html += '<a href="javascript:FileBrowser.move()">
        <i class="fa fa-share"></i> Move</a>';
      html += '<a href="javascript:FileBrowser.del()">
        <i class="fa fa-times"></i> Delete</a>';
      fileArea.innerHTML = html;
```

```
        });
      } else {
        fileArea.innerHTML = '';
      }
    }
```

The next addition to the function is a button that is shown only if a picture is selected. At this point (when we have four buttons), it is good to make some changes in the layout to get all the buttons in one line. So far, the links were the `block` elements and making them `inline-block` solves the problem. The following screenshot shows the result:

Loading a new page for the selected image

Similar to the other three links, the new one calls a function of the global `FileBrowser` object— `FileBrowser.viewImage`:

```
api.viewImage = function() {
  window.open('image.html?file=' + api.csf,
    '_blank', 'width=600,height=400');
}
```

Preferably, open the image in a new window. To do this, use the `window.open` method. This function is available in every browser. It simply loads a specific file/URL in a newly created pop up. As shown in the preceding code, the page that will be shown is stored in file called `image.html`. Also the picture's path is sent as a GET parameter and we will read it later. The following is the code in the new file:

```
<!DOCTYPE html>
<html lang="en">
    <head>
        <meta charset="utf-8">
        <title>FileBrowser</title>
```

```
        <link rel="stylesheet" href="css/styles.css">
        <script src="js/imageviewer.js"></script>
    </head>
    <body>
      <div class="image-viewer">
            <img src="" />
            <div class="dimension"></div>
      </div>
    </body>
</html>
```

There are only two things on the page. An empty `<img>` tag and an empty `<div>` tag, which will display the dimensions of the picture. We should mention that this new page has nothing to do with the `index.html` file and the `Tree` class, which we used so far. It's a completely new section controlled by another JavaScript file — `imageviewer.js`.

Showing the image and its dimensions

There are two difficulties we have to solve. They are as follows:

- The picture's path is sent via the page's URL, so we should get it from there.
- The picture's dimensions can be read from a client-side JavaScript, but only if the image is fully loaded. So, we will use Node.js.

The `imageviewer.js` file will contain a class similar to the `scripts.js` file.

```javascript
var sizeOf = require('image-size'),
    fs = require('fs'),
    path = require('path');

var ImageViewer = function() {
  var api = {};
  // ...
  return api;
}

var Viewer;
window.onload = function() {
  Viewer = ImageViewer();
}
```

At the start of the file, we defined the Node.js modules we are going to use, `fs` and `path`, which have been discussed throughout this chapter. However, `image-size` is a new module. It accepts an image path and returns its width and height. It's not a native Node.js module, so we have to include it in our `package.json` file.

```
{
  "name": "FileBrowser",
  "main": "index.html",
  "window": {
    "toolbar": true,
    "width": 690,
    "height": 900
  },
  "dependencies": {
    "image-size": "0.2.3"
  }
}
```

The node-webkit app runtime uses the same dependency format, and we have to call `npm install` to get the module installed in a local node_modules directory. Also, keep in mind that the application's packing at the end should include the node_modules folder. Once everything is set up, we are ready to show the selected picture. That's achieved with the following code:

```
var filePath = decodeURI(location.search.split('file=')[1]);
if(fs.existsSync(path.normalize(filePath))) {
  var img = document.querySelector('.image-viewer img');
  img.setAttribute('src', 'file://' + filePath);
  var dimensions = sizeOf(filePath);
  document.querySelector('.dimension').innerHTML = 'Dimension: ' +
dimensions.width + 'x' + dimensions.height;
}
```

The `location.search` function returns the current URL of the page. We know that there is only one parameter called `file`, so we can split the string and use only the second element of the array, the parameter we are interested in. We have to use `decodeURI` because the path is URL encoded and we could receive a wrong value. For example, the interval is normally replaced by %20.

We check whether the file actually exists and determine its dimensions. The rest involves showing the image and displaying the size as a text below the <img> tag. The following screenshot shows how the window may look like:

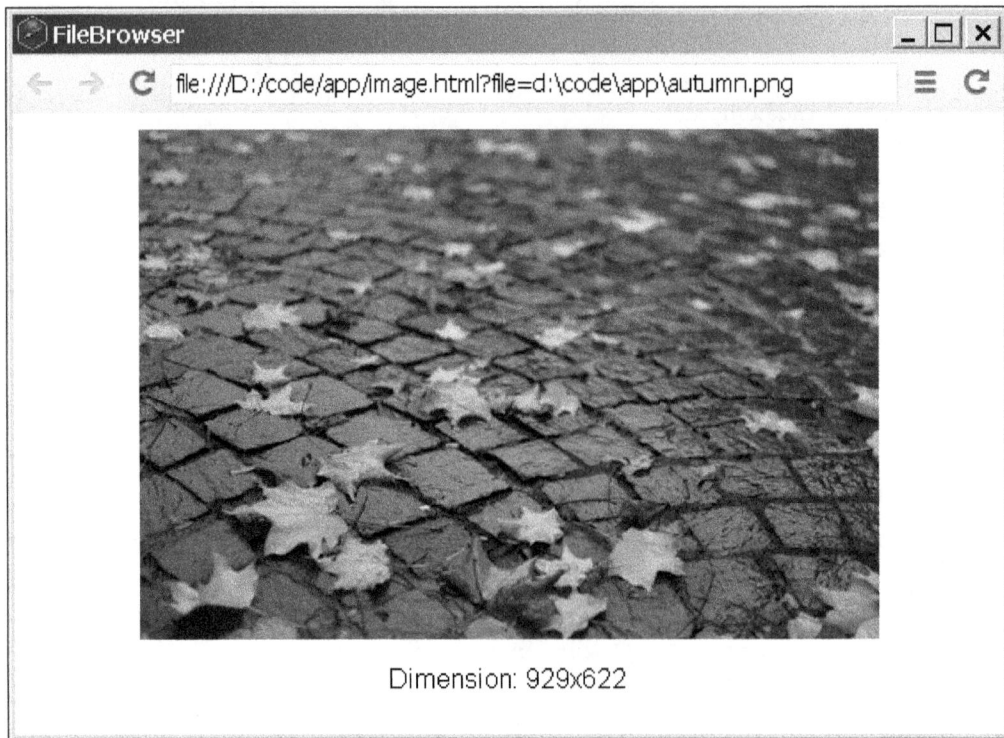

Removing the toolbar

The final thing we to do is hide the node-webkit toolbar. The user should not be able to see the currently opened file. We can do that by changing the package.json file using the following code:

```
{
  "name": "FileBrowser",
  "main": "index.html",
  "window": {
    "toolbar": false,
    "width": 690,
    "height": 900
  },
  "dependencies": {
```

```
        "image-size": "0.2.3"
    }
}
```

Setting the `toolbar` property to `false` changes our application and now it looks more like a desktop program, as shown in the following screenshot:

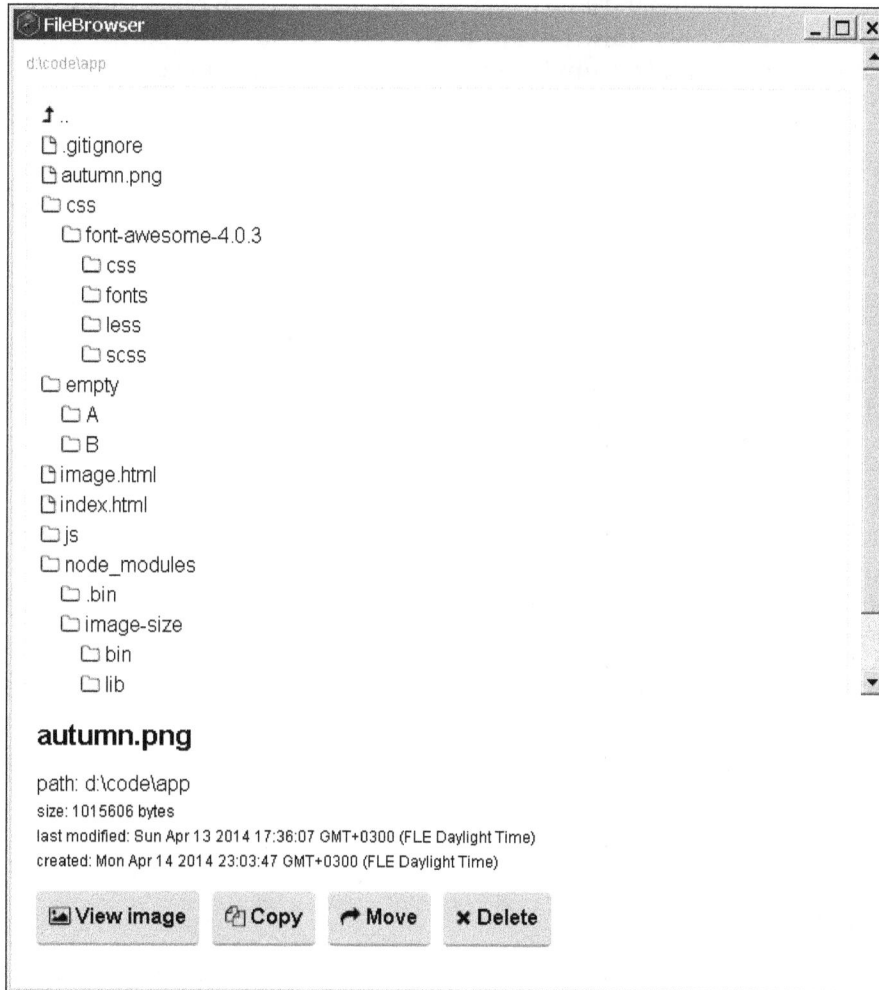

Summary

In this last chapter of the book, you learned how to build a desktop file browser with Node.js. The most interesting aspect is that we used only HTML, CSS, and JavaScript. This is because, more often than not, Node.js is used in backend development. We explored a realm of possibilities that this wonderful technology offers. It works as a command-line tool, task runner, or even wrapper for desktop applications. The big open-source community and the well-made package manager make Node.js a powerful instrument for developers around the world.

Index

benefits 189
exploring 189
Less 190
Sass 193, 194
Stylus 194, 195
current directory
modifying 229, 230
current working directory
displaying 225, 226

D

DalekJS
testing with 180-182
database
books, displaying 214
default route, adding 214
initializing 47
record, creating 212
record, deleting 213
record, editing 213
selecting 47
working with 211
data binding 43, 44
DELETE request 203
deleteToDo function 90
dependencies 82
dependencies, Ember.js
Handlebars 125
jQuery 125
dependency injection 45
dependency management 23
describe method 165
dynamic URLs
handling 34, 35

E

Ember Inspector 128
Ember.js
about 125, 126, 139
classes, exploring 126
computed properties 126, 127
controllers 131
models 130
objects, exploring 126
router 127, 128

Ember.js part
templates, defining 133, 134
writing 132
Evaluate method 177
EventEmitter 15
example-logging system 37-39
Express
about 25, 26
installing 26
installing, command-line tool used 28-32
installing, package.json file used 26, 27
URL 25
express-generator command-line tool 28

F

files
concatenating 141, 142, 154, 155
copying 230-233
deleting 230-233
displaying 226-228
ignoring 146
moving 230-233
viewing, for changes 144-146
flapi module 104
Flickr 103
Flickr.js module
writing into 111-113
Flickr protocol
authorizing 108
folder
displaying 226-228
images, obtaining from 106-108
frontend part, to-do application
files structure 92-96
to-do activities, listing 96-98
to-do lists, adding 98-101
to-do lists, deleting 100-102
to-do lists, editing 100-102
writing 92
fs module 103
functional testing 163

G

GET request 203
glob module 103

M

manifest.json 139
micro testing framework
  developing 175
middleware architecture
  exploring 20, 21
minification 143
mixins, Less
  using 190, 191
Mocha
  about 170
  example, translating 171, 172
  installing 170
  reporter, selecting 172, 173
models, Ember.js 130
Model-View-Controller (MVC)
    pattern 30, 85
modifiers 186
modular CSS
  writing 185
modules
  exploring 103
  logic, encapsulating with 44
MongoDB
  about 47, 211
  NoSQL, using with 47-50
  URL, for downloading 47
MySQL
  about 47, 211
  URL, for downloading 50
  using 50-53

N

nested definitions
  style, structuring into 192, 193
Node.js
  about 7, 25, 67, 204
  code logic, organizing in modules 10
  fundamentals 8-10
  server code, writing 69, 70
  URL 13
Node.js, task runners
  Grunt 140
  Gulp 153
Node Package Manager(npm) 23

node-webkit
  URL 219
  URL, for documentation 221
  using 219-221
NoSQL
  using, with MongoDB 47-50

O

OAuth 108
Object Oriented CSS approach. *See*
    OOCSS approach
objects, Ember.js
  exploring 126
Observer 15
online library
  developing 204
OOCSS approach
  about 187
  separate container, and content 188
  separate structure, and skin 187
open module 104
optimist module 103

P

package.json file
  used, for installing Express 26, 27
  using 104
  writing 104, 222
parts, API server
  handler 204
  responder 204
  router 204
performance tests 163
PhantomJS
  about 175
  actual test, writing 177-180
  micro testing framework, developing 175
  testing with 175
  URL 175
  working 176
POST requests 203
preprocessors 189
promise
  fulfilled state 19
  pending state 19

writing, significance 159
to-do application
  backend part 87
  creating, with Backbone.js 81
  frontend part 92
tweets
  displaying 136, 137
  obtaining, based on user handle 121-124
Twitter 117, 139

U

unit testing 162
updateFileArea function
  tweaking 234, 235
user
  transferring, to second screen 135, 136
user handle
  tweets, obtaining based on 121-124
user input
  handling 135, 136
user-to-user communication
  frontend, modifying of chat 77-79
  implementing 75
  server part, modifying 75-77

V

variables, Less
  defining 190
views, Ember.js 129

W

Webkit 175
WebSockets
  about 67
  exploring 67, 68
working directory
  current directory, modifying 229, 230
  current working directory,
    displaying 225, 226
  displaying 225
  files, copying 230-233
  files, deleting 230-233
  files, displaying 226-228
  files, moving 230-233
  folders, displaying 226-228
  using 225

Thank you for buying
Node.js Blueprints

About Packt Publishing

Packt, pronounced 'packed', published its first book "*Mastering phpMyAdmin for Effective MySQL Management*" in April 2004 and subsequently continued to specialize in publishing highly focused books on specific technologies and solutions.

Our books and publications share the experiences of your fellow IT professionals in adapting and customizing today's systems, applications, and frameworks. Our solution based books give you the knowledge and power to customize the software and technologies you're using to get the job done. Packt books are more specific and less general than the IT books you have seen in the past. Our unique business model allows us to bring you more focused information, giving you more of what you need to know, and less of what you don't.

Packt is a modern, yet unique publishing company, which focuses on producing quality, cutting-edge books for communities of developers, administrators, and newbies alike. For more information, please visit our website: www.packtpub.com.

About Packt Open Source

In 2010, Packt launched two new brands, Packt Open Source and Packt Enterprise, in order to continue its focus on specialization. This book is part of the Packt Open Source brand, home to books published on software built around Open Source licenses, and offering information to anybody from advanced developers to budding web designers. The Open Source brand also runs Packt's Open Source Royalty Scheme, by which Packt gives a royalty to each Open Source project about whose software a book is sold.

Writing for Packt

We welcome all inquiries from people who are interested in authoring. Book proposals should be sent to author@packtpub.com. If your book idea is still at an early stage and you would like to discuss it first before writing a formal book proposal, contact us; one of our commissioning editors will get in touch with you.

We're not just looking for published authors; if you have strong technical skills but no writing experience, our experienced editors can help you develop a writing career, or simply get some additional reward for your expertise.

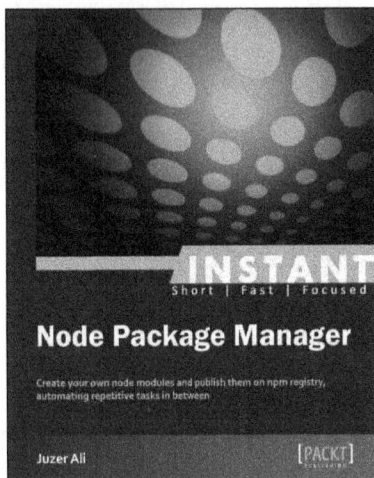

Instant Node Package Manager

ISBN: 978-1-78328-333-0   Paperback: 56 pages

Create your own node modules and publish them on npm registry, automating repetitive tasks in between

1. Learn something new in an Instant! A short, fast, focused guide delivering immediate results.

2. Create and distribute node modules.

3. Learn how to publish executables.

4. Automate the installation of dependencies.

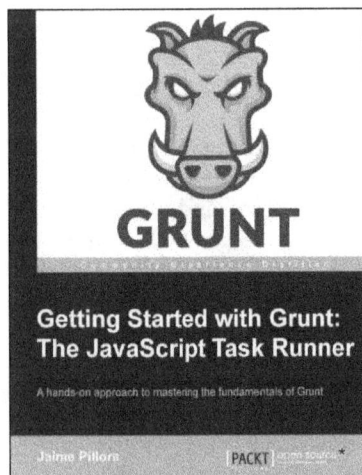

Getting Started with Grunt: The JavaScript Task Runner

ISBN: 978-1-78398-062-8   Paperback: 132 pages

A hands-on approach to mastering the fundamentals of Grunt

1. Gain insight on the core concepts of Grunt, Node.js, and npm to get started with Grunt.

2. Learn how to install, configure, run, and customize Grunt.

3. Example-driven and filled with tips to help you create custom Grunt tasks.

Please check **www.PacktPub.com** for information on our titles

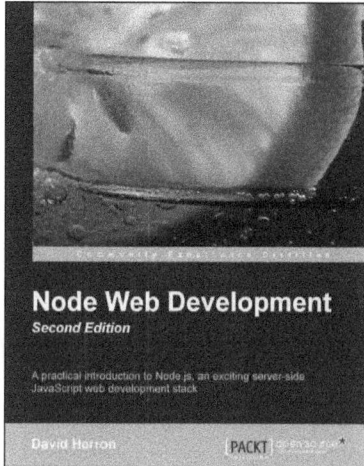

Node Web Development

Second Edition

ISBN: 978-1-78216-330-5   Paperback: 248 pages

A practical introduction to Node.js, an exciting
server-side JavaScript web development stack

1. Learn about server-side JavaScript with Node.js
   and Node modules.

2. Website development both with and without
   the Connect/Express web application
   framework.

3. Developing both HTTP server and client
   applications.

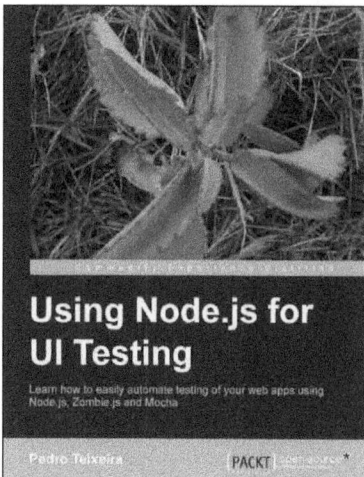

Using Node.js for UI Testing

ISBN: 978-1-78216-052-6   Paperback: 146 pages

Learn how to easily automate testing of your web
apps using Node.js, Zombie.js and Mocha

1. Use automated tests to keep your web app rock
   solid and bug-free while you code.

2. Use a headless browser to quickly test your
   web application every time you make a small
   change to it.

3. Use Mocha to describe and test the capabilities
   of your web app.